Book 2

STEEL ON STEEL

Bill Perkins

Compass Publishing
a division of
Compass International, Inc.
Coeur d'Alene, Idaho
compass.org

STEEL ON STEEL

Book 2

Compass Publishing, Inc.
Coeur d'Alene, Idaho
www.compass.org

First Printing November 2019
Printed in the United States of America.

ISBN-10: 1-57437-172-X
ISBN-13: 978-1-57437-172-7

Cover and interior design by Gordon McDonald, GoGo Design.

All proceeds from the purchase of this book go to Compass Int'l, Inc.

CONTENTS

Laurice

CONTENTS (CON'T)

PREFACE

"Iron sharpens iron, so one man sharpens another."
Prov. 27:17

Over 25 years ago we started Compass to look deeply into Scripture to best armor us for the days in which we live. Whether it's Bible prophecy, apologetics, doctrine, finances or understanding how to make the best decisions in these times, we know God's Truth sheds glorious light in every area.

The Bible has a wealth of amazing topics from which to armor ourselves for this day and hour. It's late in the game and Satan has come out of the shadows. No longer subtle, his actions are that of a desperado, wishing to take with him to eternal hell everyone he can.

Therefore, our prayer is that the "steel on steel" in this book will challenge you to think about what you believe and why you believe it. We want you to be sure your doctrines, the things that drive and guide your understanding of God's inerrant Word, are defendable.

We want you to have solid arguments to defend the accuracy of every Word God inspired.

> *"...always being ready...to give an account for the hope that is in you," 1Pet 3:15*

So enjoy this eye-opening STEEL ON STEEL - Book 2!

Note: All Scripture quotations are taken from the New American Standard Bible (NASB), and emphasis has been added by the author where underlined or bolded.

Many thanks to Susie, Tracy, Ken, Katie, Gordon and our Compass supporters for making this book possible.

Shalom!

CHAPTER ONE

TRIBULATION EVANGELISM —ON STEROIDS!

When the Church Age suddenly ends with the departure of the Holy Spirit—along with every true Believer who is indwelled by Him—it not only begins *Hell On Earth* for those left behind but will also mark the beginning of a monstrous evangelistic outreach—the likes of which the world has never seen.

The future seven-year Tribulation period will usher in the largest and most impacting sharing of the Gospel of all time. Worldwide, salvation in Jesus Christ will be offered to those who miss the Rapture via the two witnesses (Revelation 11), the 144,000 Jewish evangelists (Revelation 7 and 14) and even an angel preaching from the sky (Revelation 14:6)!

> *"And I saw another angel flying in midheaven, having an eternal gospel to preach to those who live on the earth, and to every nation and tribe and tongue and people;" Rev. 14:6*

This worldwide evangelism is a major part of the Tribulation because two main things happen during those seven horrific years:

1) People will die and go to heaven, and

2) People will die and go to hell.

The choice will not be vague ... but rather clearly delineated between:

Declining the Mark of the Beast—which is risking death as it is access to food, etc.

Accepting the Mark of the Beast—which is access to food, energy, etc., but will send the person to hell for eternity.

"...If anyone worships the beast and his image, and receives a mark on his forehead or on his hand, he also will drink of the wine of the wrath of God, which is mixed in full strength in the cup of His anger; and he will be tormented with fire and brimstone in the presence of the holy angels and in the presence of the Lamb. And the smoke of their torment goes up forever and ever; they have no rest day and night, those who worship the beast and his image, and whoever receives the mark of his name." Rev. 14:9-11

"...I saw the souls of those who had been beheaded because of their testimony of Jesus and because of the

word of God, and those who had not worshiped the beast or his image, and had not received the mark on their forehead and on their hand; and they came to life and reigned with Christ for a thousand years." Rev. 20:4

...who in their right mind wouldn't choose eternity in heaven vs. an eternity in hell?

"These will pay the penalty of eternal destruction, away from the presence of the Lord and from the glory of His power." 2Thes. 1:9

What an amazing choice! During the seven-year Tribulation, people will make the choice of eternal destiny. People end up choosing:

1) Jesus—The gift that keeps on giving, or

2) Satan—The curse that never relinquishes its hold.

Now you're probably thinking this choice is a no-brainer because who in their right mind wouldn't choose eternity in heaven vs. an eternity in hell? But today we're living in the Church Age and Believers have the benefit of being armed with the discernment of the Holy Spirit. And in the Tribulation the Holy Spirit will not indwell anyone on earth, so they'll have zero discernment.

"...[God's Holy Spirit] who now restrains will do so until he is taken out of the way." 2Thes. 2:7

Satan is the god of this earth (2 Corinthians 4:4) and Christians are already having enough trouble WITH the Restrainer being present and restraining wholesale evil. Imagine what it will be like when the earth is void of any Spirit-indwelled Believers and void of the restraining Spirit of God!

When the Rapture happens, Satan will immediately fill the void. He'll be at his best, lying about everything that just happened. I'm pretty sure he'll be making a wonderful case for joining his worldwide system, as well as his explanation of those missing from the Rapture.

...in the first few days after the Rapture, world confusion will reign.

"...he is a liar and the father of lies." John 8:44

With no God-aided discernment, choosing between food or no food will be a tough choice, even for those who may be suspicious of the World Leader's offer. Hunger can make you do stupid things.

Earth's Post-Rapture Problems

Always remember that in the first few days after the Rapture, world confusion will reign. In addition to the mass confusion and dwindling food supplies, electricity may not work.

The theory is that due to the delicacy of the electromagnetic fields between the North and South poles, if a mass exodus of humanity took place, anything electric will be out for days, if not weeks. This would mean phones, radio, TV, Internet, cars, trains, and planes immediately stop functioning.

Therefore, communication beyond the sound of your voice will be severely curtailed. *National Geographic* recently published an article on the delicate electromagnetic field surrounding the earth and the problems that would transpire if the field was disrupted. Here are a few excerpts:

> *"Many facets of our lives depend on the Earth's magnetic field, anchored by the North and South poles, from the electrical grid that powers our computers to the satellites that let us watch TV."*

> *"Our electronic grids are very tightly interconnected, so a failure in one part of it can cascade across the planet. There was a near miss in 2012 from an absolute super-storm that the sun let loose. This massive, once-in-150-years event happened to be released when the sun was facing away from our Earth. Had it been a week or two earlier, it would have been directly facing our planet and the forensic analysis suggests that we would have been sent back to the Victorian age in terms of our electrical systems had that happened."*

Our electronic grids are very tightly interconnected, so a failure in one part of it can cascade across the planet.

"Daniel Baker, director of the Laboratory for Atmospheric and Space Physics at the University of Colorado, Boulder, one of the world's experts on how cosmic radiation affects the Earth, fears that parts of the planet will become uninhabitable during a reversal. [Referring to a change in the earth's polarity] The dangers: devastating streams of particles from the sun, galactic cosmic rays, and enhanced ultraviolet B rays from a radiation-damaged ozone layer, to name just a few of the invisible forces that could harm or kill living creatures."

The Bible has for 2000 years been prophesying about the 70th Week of Daniel.

An article on undark.org said this about an electromagnetic shift:

"No lights. No computers. No cellphones. Even filling a car's gas tank would be impossible. And that's just for starters."

Of course, the Bible has for 2000 years been prophesying about the 70th Week of Daniel, the seven years of Tribulation that follow the Rapture.

"There will be signs in sun and moon and stars, and on the earth dismay among nations," Luke 21:25

Who knew *National Geographic* and other scientifically-oriented articles would be lining up so closely with the Book of Revelation! Science may catch up with the Bible after all!

The Horrific Tribulation Begins Without Warning

The contrast of before and after the Rapture couldn't be more acute. Imagine ... one second everything is normal, as it has always been. People going to work, attending a sporting event, taking kids to school, going to the store... And then in the time it takes for your eye to twinkle, utter confusion ensues. Life is drastically changed by the departing Believers.

"...in a moment, in the twinkling of an eye, ... we will be changed." 1Cor. 15:52

...no electricity, no food, no communication, no cars, no lights... nothing. It is really unimaginable.

"...we who are alive and remain will be caught up together with them in the clouds to meet the Lord in the air ..." 1Thes. 4:17

We don't know the exact date of the Rapture but do know it takes place just before the seven years of Tribulation begins. And left in its wake is no electricity, no food, no communication, no cars, no lights... nothing. It is really unimaginable.

Jesus Gave Us A Precise Template

Jesus gave us a remarkable template for the timing of events before, during, and after the Rapture. He said the days just before Rapture will be *"just like"* in the days of Noah prior to the flood and just like in the days of Lot just prior to Sodom and Gomorrah being destroyed.

> *"And **just as it happened** in the days of Noah, **so it will be** also in the days of the Son of Man: they were <u>eating</u>, they were <u>drinking</u>, they were <u>marrying</u>, they were [getting engaged/social events], until the day that Noah entered the ark, and the flood came and destroyed them all. **It was the same** as happened in the days of Lot: they were <u>eating</u>, they were <u>drinking</u>, they were <u>buying</u>, they were <u>selling</u>, they were <u>planting</u>, they were <u>building</u>; but on the day that Lot went out from Sodom it rained fire and brimstone from heaven and destroyed them all. **It will be just the same** on the day that the Son of Man is revealed." Luke 17:26-30*

As a graphic, the "days of Noah" model looks like this:

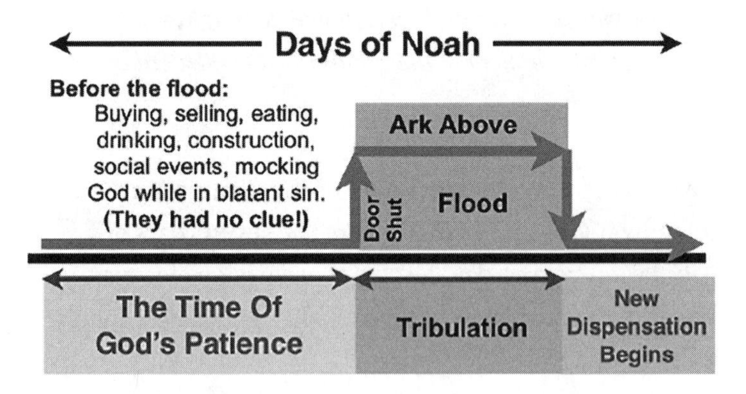

Things were normal before the flood, and then an event that had never happened, happened—rain. The rain from above and water from below the earth's crust broke through and caused a worldwide flood. Noah in his ark floated up and over the Tribulation and then returned to the earth.

Since the Rapture will be "just the same," using our template the events will look like this:

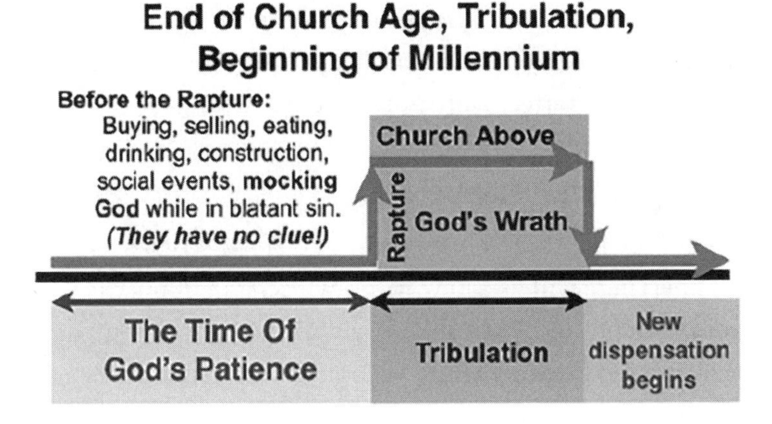

Things will be normal, then suddenly an event that has never happened will happen. The Rapture will take all Believers up and over the Tribulation below.

Those Christians who are raptured away will return seven years later to the earth to live and reign with Jesus as King of the earth.

And do notice that Jesus teaches a pre-flood doctrine, not mid-flood or post-flood! So since Jesus is pre-Trib, we should follow His example.

God's Patience Exercised Until The Rapture

Today God uses Believers to witness to non-Believers. And just like in the "days of Noah," God says He will be patient and not allow the Rapture to take place until the last of His chosen Believers are saved.

*"...when the **patience** of God kept waiting in the days of Noah, during the construction of the ark..." 1Pet. 3:20*

God's patience is amazing. Despite the ungodliness of man on earth, He is patient to delay the end of the Church Age until His perfect work is complete.

The Big "Ah-Ha" Moment

After the Rapture, as the power grid slowly comes back on line, there will be a new world with Satan filling the void with his lies. But millions will instinctively know that they missed the Holy Spirit's exodus. They may have heard the Gospel, but they didn't believe the Gospel of Jesus' shed blood as a propitiation, or payment, for their sin.

"...He loved us and sent His Son to be the propitiation for our sins." 1John 4:10

God will use many of those left behind...to be fearless evangelists.

Many who had a Biblical head-knowledge of the Gospel's doctrinal facts will immediately turn to God's Word for answers. And undoubtedly, many will come across these words:

"Those who have insight will shine brightly like the brightness of the expanse of heaven, and those who lead the many to righteousness, like the stars forever and ever." Dan. 12:3

God will use many of those left behind who knew "of God" to be fearless evangelists in the face of overwhelmingly strong Satanic opposition. Most will go to their deaths choosing Jesus at all costs.

"...I saw underneath the altar the souls of those who had been slain because of the word of God, and because of the testimony which they had maintained;" Rev. 6:9

There will be countless people who will die because they refuse to take the Mark of the Beast.

"And he causes all, the small and the great, and the rich and the poor, and the free men and the slaves, to be given a mark on their right hand or on their forehead, and he provides that no one will be able to buy or to sell, except the one who has the mark, either the name of the beast or the number of his name." Rev. 13:16-17

Does that mean some people get a second chance to be saved? No doubt, many of those left behind will be motivated by what is referred to by some as their "second chance."

But some Bible scholars erroneously teach that if people hear and reject Jesus as Savior prior to Rapture, they will not have a "second chance" to get saved in the Tribulation. They usually base this theory on these verses:

> *"...and with all the deception of wickedness for those who perish, because they did not receive the love of the truth so as to be saved.* ***For this reason God will send upon them a deluding influence so that they will believe what is false, in order that they all may be judged who did not believe the truth,*** *but took pleasure in wickedness." 2Thes. 2:10-12*

But there's no reason to believe that this means that rejecting salvation prior to Rapture seals your future in hell. That would be a blasphemous, works-oriented doctrine—salvation based on what you do or don't do. That's totally inconsistent with other "not by works" Scriptures.

Some Bible scholars erroneously teach that if people hear and reject Jesus as Savior prior to Rapture, they will not have a "second chance."

Another way to show how ridiculous that argument is: If "No second chance" is true, you could argue that because we're in the Rapture window, we should not witness any more because if someone doesn't trust Jesus now, they won't have a second chance in the Tribulation.

Obviously that dog won't hunt. We all have "second chances." How many "chances" did you have before you responded to the Gospel? Most had many. The Bible says anyone can be saved, by faith, even in the Tribulation. And millions will.

But this live-now-with-the-mark or die-without-the-mark eternal destiny choice is apparently only available during the first three and a half years of the seven-year Tribulation. In the second half of Tribulation, no one new is saved.

It's important to realize that in the first three and a half years it's the New World Leader who is in charge, and he is a man.

*"The rest of mankind, who were not killed by these plagues, did not repent of the works of their hands, so as not to worship demons, and the idols of gold and of silver and of brass and of stone and of wood, which can neither see nor hear nor walk; and they **did not repent** of their murders nor of their sorceries nor of their immorality nor of their thefts." Rev. 9:20-21*

*"Men were scorched with fierce heat; and they blasphemed the name of God who has the power over these plagues; and **they did not repent** so as to give Him glory. Rev. 16:9*

*"...they gnawed their tongues because of pain, and they blasphemed the God of heaven because of their pains and their sores; and **they did not repent** of their deeds." Rev. 16:10, 11*

World Leader vs. Satan

It's important to realize that in the first three and a half years it's the New World Leader who is in charge, and he is a man. He eventually appears to die from a head wound at the mid-point of the seven years of Tribulation. But he is miraculously healed.

> *"I saw one of his heads as if it had been slain, and his fatal wound was healed. And the whole earth was amazed and followed after the beast;" Rev. 13:3*

This is at the mid-point of the Tribulation, when Satan is kicked out of heaven and thrown to the earth.

> *"And the great dragon was thrown down, the serpent of old who is called the devil and Satan, who deceives the whole world; he was thrown down to the earth, and his angels were thrown down with him." Rev. 12:9*

Satan is an angel, a spirit, and therefore needs a body to indwell.

Satan is an angel, a spirit, and therefore needs a body to indwell, so he resurrects and empowers the body of the slain New World Leader. So it's Satan himself, indwelling the body of a man, who is ruling the earth for the last three and a half years.

After raising the New World Leader's body back to life, he stands in the Jewish Temple claiming to be God.

> *"...the man of lawlessness is revealed, the son of destruction, who opposes and exalts himself above every so-called god or object of worship, so that he takes his*

seat in the temple of God, displaying himself as being God." 2Thes. 2:3b-4

Thus begins Satan's three and a half years of "Great Tribulation" on planet earth.

"From the time that the regular sacrifice is abolished and the abomination of desolation is set up, there will be 1,290 days." Dan 12:11

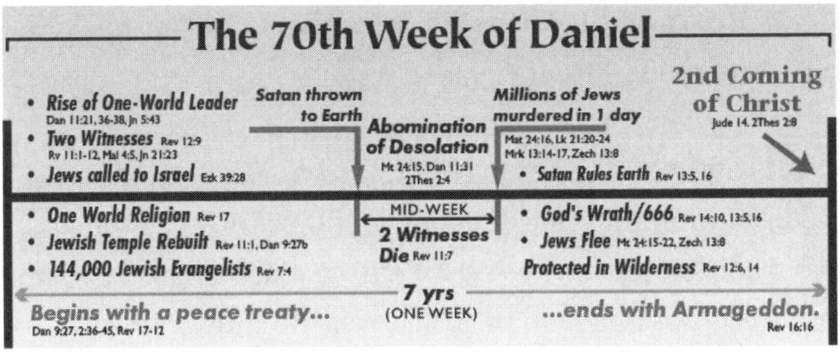

The Gospel Preached in First 3 1/2 Years of Tribulation

But in the first three and a half years of Tribulation, the eternal choice of choosing Jesus WILL be available. As outlined, the Gospel of Jesus Christ will be proclaimed throughout the world from three very unlikely sources: Two Jews, 144,000 Jews, and an Angel in the Sky.

1) Two Jewish Men

Amidst the world's utter post-rapture confusion, two ancient Jewish men will cause quite a stir by abruptly showing up again in Israel ...oddly dressed in sackcloth.

> *"And I will grant authority to my two witnesses, and they will prophesy for twelve hundred and sixty days, clothed in sackcloth." Rev. 11:3*

They will get worldwide attention because they have heavenly powers at their discretion.

> *"These have the power to shut up the sky, so that rain will not fall during the days of their prophesying; and they have power over the waters to turn them into blood, and to strike the earth with every plague, as often as they desire." Rev. 11:6*

One of the witnesses is Elijah, for whom the Jews have been waiting to return for some 2600 years. Even today, it's tradition for Jews to set an empty place at the Passover table each year for Elijah, just in case he shows up.

> *"Behold, I am going to send you Elijah the prophet before the coming of the great and terrible day of the LORD." Mal. 4:5*

Before the Passover dinner begins each year, Jewish families send their children to open the front door to see if Elijah is there. So it will not be too surprising to the Jews when Elijah eventually shows up.

They also know Elijah has yet to die as he was removed from the earth in a "chariot of fire" (an unidentified flying object—a UFO!).

> *"As they were going along and talking, behold, there appeared a chariot of fire and horses of fire which separated the two of them. And Elijah went up by a whirlwind to heaven." 2 Kings 2:11*

So when Elijah shows up again on the earth, it will be a game-changer for the Jews. Accompanying Elijah will be John the Revelator. I believe the second witness is John because:

- Moses has already died and been buried by God.
- Enoch was not a Jew, born prior to Abraham.
- Jesus, in a discussion of how the disciples would die, scolded Peter to not be concerned if John didn't die until the end of time (John 21:21-23).
- The Bible says John MUST prophesy again before "many peoples and nations and tongues and kings" (Revelation 10:11). This is an unfulfilled prophecy that will be fulfilled during the first three and a half years of the Tribulation.
- We have solid evidence of how all the other Apostles died but nothing on how John died. "Tradition" says he died in Ephesus or Patmos or wherever.

- The Roman Emperor Domitian tried to kill John by boiling him alive in oil, but he miraculously emerged unscathed. [https://www.born-again-christian.info/answers/was-the-apostle-john-boiled-in-oil.htm]

These two Jewish witnesses will die after Satan is thrown to earth in the middle of the Tribulation.

> *"When they have finished their testimony, the beast that comes up out of the abyss [Satan] will make war with them, and overcome them and kill them." Rev. 11:7*

But the three and a half years they spend on earth will be a royal pain in the side of the New World Leader. He will loathe them as they preach the gospel while at the same time calling all the Jews to come home to Israel.

2) 144,000 Jewish Witnesses

The 144,000 Jewish Witnesses also show up just after the Rapture.

> *"These are the ones who have not been defiled with women, for they have kept themselves chaste. These are the ones who follow the Lamb wherever He goes." Rev. 14:4*

These are most likely from the Rabbinical ranks of young Jewish men today who will not touch a woman until after they marry. They literally spend their days voraciously studying and debating the Old Testament.

Jesus will put His special mark on 144,000 of them. He then meets with them personally on Mount Zion where they will undoubtedly have an amazing "come to Jesus" moment.

He then meets with them where they will have an amazing "come to Jesus" moment.

The veil will lift and their eyes will be opened to truth. They'll make the stunning connection that they murdered their Messiah. This new knowledge from the Lord will propel them into an evangelistic fervor that will cover the earth.

"And I looked, and behold, the Lamb was standing on Mount Zion, and with Him one hundred and forty-four thousand, having His name and the name of His Father written on their foreheads." Rev. 14:1

It's interesting that today, the top of Mt. Zion in Jerusalem has never been fully developed. It encompasses two gentile cemeteries, and the whole area is capable of holding a crowd of 144,000 to meet Jesus personally. Or maybe in groups of 12,000. Scripture is unclear, but there is plenty of room on the top of Mt. Zion.

With their Biblical knowledge of the Old Testament, hearing the rest of the story will make total sense as Jesus is hidden many places in the Old Testament Scriptures. They'll immediately devour the New Testament as well. And don't miss the irony of so many Jews embracing Jesus the Messiah, whom for centuries they've rejected!

3) An Angel in the Sky

Last on this list of three ways God proclaims the Gospel in the Tribulation is through an angel who witnesses in the sky.

I've often taught in Bible studies, "In the Church Age, God doesn't send an angel in the sky on Wednesday nights to tell the world to worship Him, but rather, He uses Believers on this earth to witness one-on-one."

Well, with the Believers and the Holy Spirit gone, God ***will*** send an angel in the sky!

> *"And I saw another angel flying in midheaven, having an eternal gospel to preach to those who live on the earth, and to every nation and tribe and tongue and people; and he said with a loud voice, 'Fear God, and give Him glory, because the hour of His judgment has come; worship Him who made the heaven and the earth and sea and springs of waters.'" Rev. 14:6-7*

First, do notice that God's "creation," not "evolution," is part of this angelic proclamation! If for no other reason, heaven will be a wonderful place because the wicked lie of evolution will have been exposed and the creative genius of God revealed in abundant glory!

But the thought of an angel preaching the Gospel from the sky is amazing. Wonder how he accounts for the different time zones?

Regardless, during the first half of the Tribulation, the world will be teeming with the option to either choose long-term Heaven via Jesus' death, burial, and resurrection (but likely be killed) or short-term "heaven," temporary food from Satan, and wail forever in hell.

It's a terrible time, but God promises Believers that we'll miss it as we're not destined for wrath.

> *"For God has not destined us for wrath, but for obtaining salvation through our Lord Jesus Christ," 1Thes. 5:9*

The thought of an angel preaching the Gospel from the sky is amazing.

The coming Rapture, the stunning conclusion to the Church Age, will remove Believers from God's wrath. Those left behind will have the opportunity to trust Jesus, and an uncountable number will, but it will be quite physically painful.

"After these things I looked, and behold, a great multitude which no one could count, from every nation and all tribes and peoples and tongues, standing before the throne and before the Lamb, clothed in white robes, and palm branches were in their hands;" Rev. 7:9

"....These who are clothed in the white robes, who are they, and where have they come from?...he said to me, 'these are the ones who come out of the great tribulation, and they have washed their robes and made them white in the blood of the Lamb.'" Rev. 7:13

A total of half the world population dies...

"They shall hunger no more, nor thirst anymore; nor will the sun beat down on them, nor any heat; ...God will wipe every tear from their eyes." Rev. 7:16-17

The Seven Years of Tribulation will be horrible. Here are only a FEW of the problems:

- One fourth of the earth dies from disease and raging nuclear wars (Revelation 6:4,8) in the beginning, then another one third of mankind dies a few years later. A total of half the world population dies in the first 3 1/2 years. And then it get really bad in the second half — which ends with only a few surviving! (Isaiah 24:6).

- Everything living in the sea dies (Revelation 16:3).
- The economy is devastated by runaway inflation (Revelation 6:5,6).
- There is no escape from the horrible heat (Revelation 16:9).
- Satan's worst demons that have been bound up since Noah's flood will be released into the earth ... again (Revelation 9:2,3)!

Based on the Bible's many prophecies about this time period, we're obviously getting very close. We need to be asking the Lord daily for opportunities to share what He has done in our life with our family, friends, and co-workers.

You can download a free booklet, *Millions Missing?—What to do if you miss the Rapture!* at **compass.org**. It's good to leave lying around!

CHAPTER TWO

THE BIBLE AND CAPITALISM

Our public schools have for 40 years pooh-poohed capitalism and elevated socialism to the point that today surveys show an astonishing 35% of Americans, and the majority of our youth, think socialism is better than capitalism!

<u>Humanistic Worldview</u>

Man is born good.
Man is the standard.
Environment causes behavior.
Rights come from the government.

This movement defies logic, is built on lies, and worst of all is anti-Biblical.

Today's youth have a distorted view of how our country works and need to wake up and smell the coffee. There's no free lunch. Biblical capitalism works. Socialism, communism, fascism or whatever label you put on it, doesn't.

The United States, founded on Biblical capitalism, has produced the wealthiest and most productive country in the history of mankind.

Only recently have we regressed a bit due to implementation of humanistic socialist policies.

Biblical Worldview

Man is born sinful/needs Savior.
Bible is the standard.
Man is responsible for behavior.
Rights come from God.

Biblical capitalism is built on freedom as its centerpiece. The greater the freedom, the greater the wealth. On the opposite side—the greater the government, the greater the poverty.

In a recent presidential primary, Bernie Sanders garnered a lot of votes touting socialism. But he literally had to tell half-truths to make socialism sound good. For anyone who looks at the facts, socialism tries to make everyone equal regardless of individual effort. That has proven over and over not to work.

Socialistic Countries' Disasters

The once-mighty USSR fell apart in 1989 due to iron-fisted socialistic policies that destroyed the economy while taking away virtually ALL freedoms from its citizens.

People who have visited Cuba say it's like time stopped in 1959 when Castro and communism took over. Literally all the cars on the road were manufactured in, or before, 1959. (The photo on page 26 is a recent picture taken in Cuba.) Unemployment is 48%, and 80% of those who have jobs work for the government, making Cuba's economy a disaster.

Venezuela is an even bigger disaster. Their hospitals are germ-infested trash dumps, and they're rioting over food. In less than 20 years they've gone from the most prosperous South American nation to the poorest—all because they elected a socialistic government that did away with capitalistic policies.

North and South Korea are perfect examples of the difference between Biblical capitalism (freedom) and communism (slavery). In communist North Korea, 2.5 million people starve each year. In capitalistic South Korea, the GDP is the 10th largest in the world.

What About the Scandinavian Countries?

Often people try to use the Scandinavian countries, like Sweden, to show how socialism can work today. But they are NOT Democratic socialist countries. In the Scandinavian countries, the means of production are primarily owned by private individuals, not the government.

For instance, Denmark has a market-based

Top 25 Most Globalized countries, 2015

1. Ireland 91.30	7. Denmark 86.30	13. Czech Republic	19. UK 82.96
2. Netherlands 91.24	8. Portugal 86.29	14. Spain 83.71	20. France 82.65
3. Belgium 91.00	9. Switzerland 86.04	15. Luxembourg 83.56	21. Australia 81.64
4. Austria 90.24	10. Finland 85.64	16. Cyprus 83.54	22. Italy 79.51
5. Singapore 87.49	11. Hungary 85.49	17. Slovak Republic 83.52	23. Poland 79.43
6. Sweden 86.59	12. Canada 85.03	18. Norway 83.30	24. Estonia 79.35
			25. Greece 79.08

CEOWORLD MAGAZINE Source: 2015 KOF Index of Globalization

economy that embraces global capitalism and free trade (as does Sweden). They have no minimum wage, and wages vary depending on the industry. They have school choice using public money in the form of vouchers that citizens can use for private schools. And some of the most successful private schools are FOR PROFIT!

Socialism is simply a camouflaged steppingstone to communism.

Why Socialism Doesn't Work

Socialism doesn't work because it takes income away from productive people and gives it to non-productive people. When a percentage of your hard-earned money is confiscated, you have fewer choices and a lower standard of living. If all your money is confiscated, you're a slave.

Socialism is simply a camouflaged steppingstone to communism. We should never abandon the Biblical principles on which our nation was founded, lest we forever lose our remaining liberties.

Margaret Thatcher

Margaret Thatcher, Prime Minister of Great Britain from 1979 to 1990, summed up socialism nicely:

"The problem with socialism is that you eventually run out of other people's money."

Government doesn't produce, it only consumes. A past staunch capitalistic President said it best:

> *"Government is not a solution to our problems, government IS the problem... Government does not solve problems, it subsidizes them. Government's view of the economy could be summed up in a few short phrases: If it moves, tax it. If it keeps moving, regulate it. If it stops moving, subsidize it. The problem is not that people are taxed too little, the problem is that government spends too much." — Ronald Reagan*

So Bernie Sanders and his "Feel the Bern" embracement of socialism is full of lies and mis-truths. Millennials again need to wake up and learn capitalist facts.

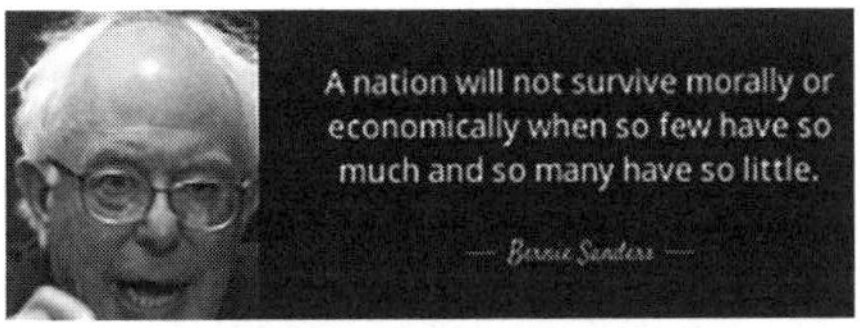

The Basics of Biblical Capitalism

It's important to understand the basics of Biblical capitalism, its roots, and its basis for providing workers with liberty and motivation. So let's first look at the very beginning.

> *"Then the LORD God took the man and put him into the garden of Eden to cultivate it (Lit. "work it") and keep it." Gen. 2:15*

As part of the original creation, work (stewardship) was considered "good," and performed by the man. But with

Adam's sin, work was corrupted along with everything else.

> *"Cursed is the ground because of you; in toil [lit. "pain and sorrow"] you will eat of it all the days of your life... By the sweat of your face you will eat bread, till you return to the ground ..." Gen 3:17b, 19*

Because of Adam's sin, a new dispensation began and every man had to work hard, toil, just to eat...and had to do this <u>all the days of his life</u>. There is no getting around this. You are commanded by God to work until you "return to the ground," meaning when you die.

So working "all the days of your life" means retirement is unBiblical. You should never plan to reach a point in life where you stop working. It's certainly Biblical to save money so you can share with your family and others as God would reveal and have the option to change what you do later in life. But you should never make "retirement" your savings goal.

Applying this in the Church Age, Paul was quite clear:

> *"...if anyone is not willing to work, then he is not to eat, either." 2Thes. 3:10*

> *"Now such persons we command and exhort in the Lord Jesus Christ to <u>work</u> in quiet fashion and eat their own bread." 2Thes. 3:12*

The Bible says hunger is a motivator to work. If you take away hunger, you take away a major motivator.

> *"A worker's appetite works for **him**, for his hunger urges him on." Prov. 16:26*

Therefore, it's incumbent for the **man** of the house to work for wages and be the provider for his family. Other than temporary circumstances where you might use your unemployment insurance that you purchased to temporarily tide you over (or Workers' Comp), there is no reason to be dependent on the government for money.

> *"The hand of the diligent will rule, but the slack hand will be put to forced labor." Prov. 12:24*

The U.S. Social Program Quagmire

Yet in the last 70 years we've moved from our Biblical roots and have begun socialistic welfare programs to help those who, for whatever reason, have no housing or food.

Based on the off-balance idea that we need to protect the rights of people to have higher education, housing, and food, liberals have passed legislation that began instituting socialistic policies—forcibly taking from those who have and giving it to those who don't.

Food stamps, now called "Electronic Benefits Transfer Card" (EBT), HUD Section 8 housing, SNAP, and other programs have been added through the years ENABLING people NOT to work. By having endless programs that reward people for not working, we have abandoned the Biblical principles that made this nation great and that even threaten its continued existence.

"The soul of the sluggard craves and gets nothing, but the soul of the diligent is made fat." Prov. 13:4

We have abandoned the Biblical principles that made this nation great...

However, allowing the government to take over as the provider-god has not helped in the long run because it's made people dependent on handouts. This sends a not-so-subtle message that the government is more important than God.

Americans no longer look to God to solve their problems; rather, they look to the government.

"There is nothing better for a man than to eat and drink and tell himself that his labor is good." Eccl. 2:24a

Concurrently we have kicked God out of the classroom, avoided teaching Biblical principles, and are attempting to erase all religious symbols in public places. And there's a price to pay when you go Satan's way instead of God's way.

"But if anyone does not provide for his own, and especially for those of his household, he has denied the faith and is worse than an unbeliever." 1Tim. 5:8

If there's nothing better than to work, then there's nothing worse than to not work. Every male Believer has read and understood the commandment to "provide for his own." (1 Timothy 5:8)

God's truth is written on the heart of every non-Believer, too. People on government handouts intrinsically know that they are in an ever-deepening hole.

But they are told they have been discriminated against... so they have to blame someone. "It's not your fault you're poor, it's ____ fault." This solves nothing and only adds misery on top of misery. The government is not dealing with the root problem—which is abandoning the Biblical principles of capitalism and the benefits of hard work.

Money is NOT Evil!

Socialists are attacking our tried-and-true system—making "accumulation of money" an evil pursuit. Legally earned money is not evil, regardless of how much you make or save. It's the LOVE of money that trips people up... when you make money your god.

"For the ***love*** *of money is a root of all sorts of evil, and some by longing for it have wandered away from the faith and pierced themselves with many griefs." 1Tim. 6:10*

"Better is a little with righteousness than great income with injustice." Prov. 16:8

I recently counseled with a Christian (supposedly) man who was divorcing his wife for the expressed purpose of saving money. I pointed out all the Biblical reasons for not divorcing his wife, including the impact on his kids. But he said he "had to do what is right for him." He had made money his god. And when you choose money over God, it's only downhill from there.

"For they exchanged the truth of God for a lie, and worshiped and served the creature rather than the Creator..." Rom. 1:25

It All Comes from God

The key is to understand that all income is a gift from the Lord.

"...moreover, that every man who eats and drinks sees good in all his labor —it is the gift of God." Eccl. 3:13

God gives you the ability to work, the mind to think, and the strength to do the job. Your job is to work hard. It's God's call whether you're wealthy. It's imperative to always keep this in perspective.

"...remember the LORD your God, for it is He who is giving you power to make wealth," Deut. 8:18

> *"It is the blessing of the LORD that makes rich, and He adds no sorrow to it." Prov. 10:22*

Our work emphasis and motivation should be on doing a good job, providing a quality product, satisfying a need, etc., not on getting rich.

> *"Do not weary yourself to gain wealth, cease from your consideration of it. When you set your eyes on it, it is gone. For wealth certainly makes itself wings like an eagle that flies toward the heavens." Prov. 23:4-5*

> *"It is vain for you to rise up early, to retire late, to eat the bread of painful labors; for He gives to His beloved even in his sleep." Psa. 127:2*

> *"He who loves money will not be satisfied with money, nor he who loves abundance with its income." Eccl. 5:10*

> *"Instruct those who are rich in this present world not to be conceited or to fix their hope on the uncertainty of riches, but on God, who richly supplies us with all things to enjoy." 1Tim. 6:17*

> *"No one can serve two masters; for either he will hate the one and love the other, or he will be devoted to one and despise the other. You cannot serve God and wealth." Matt. 6:24*

Profit Is Not a Dirty Word

Profit is not a "necessary evil." It's part of the first rule of business—which is "your net income must exceed your net costs." Some call that profit, but I call it the first rule of survival. You can't stay in business unless you mark up your products or services by reasonable margins to make a profit. Profit allows you to stay in business; otherwise you can't keep the lights on.

God doesn't think "profit" is evil because He speaks positively about making a profit—even promising Israel He will teach them how to "profit."

> *"... I am the LORD your God, who teaches you to profit, who leads you in the way you should go." Isa. 48:17*

> ***God doesn't think "profit" is evil because He speaks positively about making a profit.***

> *"In all labor there is profit, but mere talk leads only to poverty." Prov. 14:23*

Lending and Borrowing are not Evil

God also said He would make Israel a lender to many nations, but not borrowers.

> *"The LORD will open for you His good storehouse, the heavens, to give rain to your land in its season and to bless all the work of your hand; and you shall lend to many nations, but you shall not borrow." Deut. 28:12*

If lending isn't a sin, then obviously this means borrowing is not a sin either... you just have to be extremely careful as there is a huge downside if things don't work out.

"Do not be among those who give pledges, among those who become guarantors for debts. If you have nothing with which to pay, why should he take your bed from under you?" Prov. 22:26-27

Five Benefits of Working Hard in Order to Profit

"Commit your way to the LORD, trust also in Him, and He will do it." Psa. 37:5

Commit your way to the LORD, trust also in Him...

1) You'll be happier.

"When you shall eat of the fruit of your hands, you will be happy and it will be well with you." Psa. 128:2

"Not that I speak from want, for I have learned to be content in whatever circumstances I am. I know how to get along with humble means, and I also know how to live in prosperity; in any and every circumstance I have learned the secret of being filled and going hungry, both of having abundance and suffering need." Phil. 4:11-12

2) You'll always have enough.

"I have been young and now I am old, yet I have not seen the righteous forsaken or his descendants begging bread." Psa. 37:25

"He who tills his land will have plenty of bread," Prov. 12:11a

"Make sure that your character is free from the love of money, being content with what you have;" Heb.13:5

3) Hard work is a witness.

"Let your light shine before men in such a way that they may see your good works, and glorify your Father who is in heaven." Matt. 5:16

"Do you see a man skilled in his work? He will stand before kings; he will not stand before obscure men." Prov. 22:29

4) There is the possibility of financial gain.

"Let the favor of the Lord our God be upon us; and confirm for us the work of our hands; yes, confirm the work of our hands." Psa. 90:17

"The hard-working farmer ought to be the first to receive his share of the crops." 2Tim. 2:6

"Poor is he who works with a negligent hand, but the hand of the diligent makes rich." Prov. 10:4

5) You can share with those in need.

"...he must labor, performing with his own hands what is good, so that he will have something to share with one who has need." Eph. 4:28

"He who is generous will be blessed, for he gives some of his food to the poor." Prov. 22:9

God Is your Ultimate Employer

> *"Whatever you do, do your work heartily, as for the Lord rather than for men, knowing that from the Lord you will receive the reward of the inheritance. It is the Lord Christ whom you serve." Col. 3:23-24*

I have always said that if you want to be successful working for someone else, tell them you will work free for a week to show them what you can do. Then, consider your employer is actually giving you orders from Jesus Christ. If Jesus is personally giving you orders, through your employer, you should break doors down doing what He says. You would get there early and stay late, making sure your ultimate employer (Jesus) is getting more than His money's worth. If you work like this, you'll have a job forever at top pay.

Should You Work for Yourself?

For many, being independent (owning your own business) gives you the best opportunity to earn a good living. Entrepreneurship is not for everyone, but instead of making someone else successful, entrepreneurs make themselves successful—and keep the profits! You're paid exactly what you deserve.

The capitalistic free enterprise system in the United States encourages ambition, incentive, competition, and hard work. If you are willing to work hard to reach your dreams, you have that opportunity.

Success Is Not a Sure Thing

Starting a business is not that hard, but making a profit takes a lot of work—especially in the early stages. Some 20% of small businesses fail within the first year. Half last only five years. And only a third last 10 years or longer.

Your best chance with a non-franchised business is when you have a compelling desire to make something work. Whether your motivation is feeding your family, increasing your income for a larger house, or trying to prove that a business or service will work, you need a compelling incentive to carry you through the hard times.

There are also structured franchise opportunities. These tried-and-true businesses have track records of success and are looking for someone to instruct what to do to be successful.

Whether you're in food service, health care, real estate, or any of the myriads of other areas, if you have the start-up cash, you can be your own boss and have a higher likelihood of success—especially if you operate your business with Biblical principles.

> *"This is a trustworthy statement; and concerning these things I want you to speak confidently, so that those who have believed God will be careful to engage in good deeds. These things are good and profitable for men." Titus 3:8*

Hobby Lobby and Chick-fil-A are businesses that have stood their ground using the Bible to guide their business decisions and have done quite well. There are tens of thousands of smaller mom-and-pop businesses doing the same thing, working hard using Biblical principles and trusting God to provide.

> *"Commit your works to the LORD and your plans will be established." Prov. 16:3*

There is a long-time Compass supporter who operates very successful franchises across the United States. He's committed to God's Biblical principles in everything he does. Amazingly, his business plan provides his company with zero revenue unless the franchisee is profitable. So he is quite motivated to make his franchises successful, and they are!

> *"Entrepreneurs and their small enterprises are responsible for almost all the economic growth in the United States." —Ronald Reagan*

If capitalism moves one toward the Bible and socialism does not, then the chart below makes a simple but pointed statement:

	Democrat	Republican	
SATAN	**Socialism**	**Capitalism**	GOD
	Slavery	Freedom	

Republican vs. Democrat
Capitalism vs. Socialism
Christian vs. Atheist
God vs. Satan

Government	Smaller better	Larger better
Assets	Owned by private businesses	Owned by government
Wages	Determined by market	Set by government
Prices	By Supply and Demand	By Government
Taxes	Lower = less gov't spending	Higher = more gov't spending
Healthcare	Free market	Government controlled
Abortion	Pro-life / pre-born is a person	Pro-death /pre-born no rights
Gun Control	Pro 2nd Amendment	Anti 2nd Amendment
Homosexual	Biblical view	Anti-biblical view
Religion	Pro Bible	Anti-Bible

The bottom line is that the opposite of socialism/slavery/Satan is capitalism/freedom/God. God has allowed a free enterprise system in the United States, and it encourages ambition, competition, and hard work with a monetary incentive.

"Whatever your hand finds to do, do it with all your might;" Eccl. 9:10

"Delight yourself in the LORD; and He will give you the desires of your heart." Psa. 37:4

Not only should you never take our great capitalistic system for granted, you're going to have to defend it too—

to the youth today whom we refer to as the Millennials who have been poorly taught economics.

And since the Bible says our real enemy is not flesh and blood, I must call a spade a spade: This movement to take apart our Judeo-Christian capitalistic system is straight from Satan—straight from the pit of hell.

So it's time to put on the full-armor big-boy pants the next time someone talks positively about socialism and exhort them with some capitalistic verses from the Bible.

CHAPTER THREE

THE HOLE IN YOUR HEART

More and more, men and women in high positions of influence are being revealed to be liars and/or being caught in deplorable and degrading sin. Why is God suddenly allowing us to see the depths of our political corruption and the astonishing sinfulness of powerful men? What is causing this?

The answer is embedded in the Bible for all to see. But most people aren't willing to look for eternal answers and instead only wish to deal with the here and now, to their own peril.

Where to Start

For Believers, we look at problems and solutions from a Biblical perspective—temporal vs. eternal. God's way vs. man's way.

> *"Set your mind on the things above, not on the things that are on earth." Col. 3:2*

Sin today is exacerbated by the explosion of pornography. An unbelievable number of men, both Christian and non-Christian, have fallen to Satan's "lust of the eyes" lures, damaging—or breaking completely— their marriages.

God warns us to be careful about what we allow our eyes to view.

> *"The eye is the lamp of your body; when your eye is clear, your whole body also is full of light; but when it is bad, your body also is full of darkness." Luke 11:34*

It's probable that most, if not all, of the national leaders who are being busted for sex innuendos or actions outside of marriage have had, or are having, problems with pornography.

The Roots of Sin

When Adam was created, he was designed perfectly, with a place for God to live in his heart, to have perfect union with the Creator of the universe. He walked and conversed with God, having a personal and direct relationship.

But when Adam sinned, God, being perfect and having no alternative, had to withdraw from that relationship. Sin had caused Adam to lose what was originally designed for him—having God's Spirit living in his heart. Adam was left with what Blaise Pascal called "A heart-shaped vacuum."

That godless, sinful condition that Adam now embodied, with a heart-shaped vacuum that only God can fill, was passed along to every living human being on the earth through the male.

In fact, if a female could have a baby without a human male being involved, she could have a sinless offspring—which is how Jesus was born sinless, not having a human father.

Everyone since Adam has been born with this vacuum, a hole in the heart. Each person has a place designed for God, but because of sin, God cannot live there. So man, realizing he is missing something, spends his life trying to fill his heart-hole with temporal things.

The Problem with a Hole in Our Heart

...if a female could have a baby without a human male being involved, she could have a sinless offspring...

The sin nature and the drive to fill that empty heart is difficult for humans to control. No matter what humans try to fill their empty hearts with, it is only temporarily satisfying. More and more earthly "things" have to be continually inserted.

Jesus even commented that rich people are the hardest to reach because they have the money for an endless supply of temporal items. If they got tired of filling their heart-hole with one thing, they had the money to switch to another. And then another.

So it didn't take long for Satan to lead the earth in open rebellion. It got so bad that God had to basically start over by wiping out the earth with a global Flood. Thankfully God saved Noah, the only one righteous man left on earth, and his family.

Post Flood, God restrained many of the worst of Satan's angels and allowed the earth's humans to repopulate. But humans still have the same problem. They are designed with a place for God in their hearts, but God, being absolutely perfect, could not indwell His human creation because mankind was sinful.

God loved us so much that He came from heaven in order to provide a way out...

Thankfully God loved us so much that He came from heaven in order to provide a way out of this sinful condition in which man was seemingly forever trapped. God became a human in order to redeem mankind from this sinful condition.

"And the Word became flesh, and dwelt among us," John 1:14a

God lived a sinless life on earth and allowed His blood to be shed while dying as a sacrifice for a full and complete atonement for our sin, thus defeating death. This atonement broke down the barrier between God and man. God could again commune with His human creation.

God's Rules Rule

But receiving the atonement from God to escape the hot, dark, and forever fires of hell has a condition attached. You must personally believe the Gospel news, trusting that God's death on the Cross and His subsequent resurrection did in fact pay for your personal sins—past, present, and future.

> *"...if you confess with your mouth Jesus as Lord, and believe in your heart that God raised Him from the dead, you will be saved;"* Rom. 10:9

For those of us who do confess to being a sinner in need of a Savior and believe that God paid for our sins, the Lord comes into our hearts to live permanently and forever refilling our heart-shaped vacuum, completely satisfying our heart-hole.

Unfortunately, in this life, we still live with our sin nature on this earth.

> *"If we say that we have no sin, we are deceiving ourselves and the truth is not in us."* 1 John 1:8

Thankfully, a born-again relationship gives us access to power over our still-existing sin nature. And ultimately, we will receive a new, sinless body for eternity in heaven.

So Believers use this new Godly access to armor up against being duped into sinning on this earth. And even though we fail in this life, the more Scriptural armor we employ, the more we mature and are less likely to fall for sin's continual lures.

"But solid food is for the mature, who because of practice have their senses trained to discern good and evil."
Heb. 5:14

The World Without God

Therefore, it is a Biblical fact that the only way on this earth to effectively deal with sin is through the shed blood of Jesus Christ. So when we're watching headlines about the sinfulness of prominent men, keep in mind that they're duped—operating in a fallen world, and not seeking the only true answer—Jesus Christ.

...the only way on this Earth to effectively deal with sin is through the shed blood of Jesus Christ.

"No wonder, for even Satan disguises himself as an angel of light."
2Cor. 11:14

When non-Believers are caught with their hands in the cookie jar, they naturally try all imaginable ways to deal with their sin nature other than turning to Jesus. They will apologize, explain, or complain that they forgot the rules. Or they gravitate to the latest "get out of jail free" card offered by Satan: "getting counsel."

Don't be fooled. Secular counseling, without using 100% Biblical principles, is from the pit of hell. Sadly, many

"Christian counselors" incorporate some secular thinking when they offer solutions. True counselors point to God's inerrant Word to show where out-of-bounds lines are clearly marked. One session should be enough.

Desiring "Self" to Be God Is Not New

In Genesis 3:1-7, Satan tempted Adam with "You can be your own God." Satan is still using that same line 6000 years later. He wants people to think only of themselves, today. He wants us to think we should be focused on ourselves in this life, not on God and eternity.

When you look at the Isaiah 14 passages regarding Satan's fall, the root characteristic of his sin was "self." Six times Satan says, or implies, "I"... Satan didn't want to worship God, he wanted to ***be*** God.

Satan didn't want to worship God, he wanted to be God.

"But you [Satan] said in your heart, 'I will ascend to heaven; I will raise my throne above the stars of God, And I will sit on the mount of assembly [I will sit] in the recesses of the north. I will ascend above the heights of the clouds; I will make myself like the Most High.'" Isaiah 14:13-14

So the answer to dealing with sin is not to rely on our human abilities and personally seek ways to climb out of our miry mess. Rather, we're to look to God. True and lasting answers are found only in His Word.

We can't, but God can. God is the only thing that will come into our lives and permanently satisfy the desires in our life and truly fill the hole in our heart.

"I Can't Get No Satisfaction"

We can easily see in the news what happens when you refuse God's will as the purpose for your life:

- Harvey Weinstein was exposed trying to put temporal sinful sex in his empty heart-hole. He can go to all the counselors he can find, but he will still have his sin nature after all of those counseling sessions. He's fighting a losing battle and nothing will change permanently, unless he turns to the Bible as his counselor.

- Matt Lauer also put self first, via sinful sex, into his empty heart-hole. He can apologize and promise to be better, but he's fighting a losing battle unless he turns to Jesus for true satisfaction.

- Charlie Rose can question the accuracy of all the accusations against him while promising to change, but he can't change unless he allows into his life the only thing that can really change him, Jesus Christ living in his empty heart-hole!

- Former comedian and Minnesota Senator Al Franken can back-pedal all he wants, but nothing will actually change until he looks to Jesus to fill the hole in his heart.

- And John Conyers, Anthony Weiner, Bill Cosby, John Edwards, Tiger Woods... the list is seemingly endless.

God seems to be telling us we need to get our eyes back on the things that matter.

And matter they do. The entire non-believing world is only a nano-second from the worst imaginable horror coming on this earth for seven full years. We have to be bold in these last days, proclaiming and defending what we know to be true.

> *"...always being ready to make a defense to everyone who asks you to give an account for the hope that is in you, yet with gentleness and reverence;" 1Pet. 3:15*

The entire non-believing world is only a nano-second away from the worst imaginable horror...

Is God allowing one last opportunity to proclaim truth to people before the final curtain closes? Maybe. So over dinner conversations with family and friends, ask the Lord to give you the opportunity to plant eternal seeds.

> *"...praying at the same time for us as well, that God will open up to us a door for the word, so that we may speak forth the mystery of Christ, for which I have also been imprisoned;" Col. 4:3*

Because "just like" in the days of Noah, the time of God's patience won't last forever.

"...when the patience of God kept waiting in the days of Noah, during the construction of the ark, in which a few, that is, eight persons, were brought safely through the water." 1Pet. 3:20

CHAPTER FOUR

CHRISTIANS AND DIVORCE

With professing Christians getting divorced at the same or higher rate than non-Christians, something is amiss in the Christian world. Percentages of Christians filing for divorce have leveled, but not dropped in the last 25 years. Desiring to get to the meat of this problem, we asked a Christian divorce attorney to speak at a *Steeling the Mind Bible Conference*. He opened a lot of eyes. More on that later.

But with such a large number of professing Christians in our churches who are divorced, what is their status? Can divorced men serve as deacons or elders? Can they teach Sunday School? Are they second-class Christians?

Is Divorce an Unpardonable Sin?

There is much confusion in the church over the "divorce" issue. Make no bones about it, divorce is horrible. God hates it. That is because God loves us, and divorce always hurts people. **Always.**

Interestingly, despite God's vehement language forbidding divorce, it was permitted under the Old Testament law.

> *"When a man takes a wife and marries her, and it happens that she finds no favor in his eyes because he has found some indecency in her, and he writes her a certificate of divorce and puts it in her hand and sends her out from his house." Deut. 24:1*

Jesus referred to that law when He said to the Pharisees, who were under the law:

Many pastors teach that if your spouse is committing sexual sin, you have permission to divorce.

> *"It was said, '**Whoever sends his wife away, let him give her a certificate of divorce**'; but I say to you that everyone who divorces his wife, except for the reason of unchastity, makes her commit adultery; and whoever marries a divorced woman commits adultery.*
> *Matt. 5:31-32*

Unfortunately, many, many pastors use that verse to teach that if your spouse is committing sexual sin, you have, from the mouth of Jesus in Scripture, permission to divorce.

But wait, does that verse apply to those of us living in the Church Age? Absolutely not! Jesus was addressing the Jews under the law, not Christians living in the Church Age. Paul, through the inspiration of the Holy Spirit, addressed Believers in the Church Age and said:

> *"Husbands, love your wives, even as Christ also loved the church, and gave himself up for her;" Eph. 5:25*

That is a hugely different Scriptural command for Believers living post-cross. Christ would never divorce the Church! So another dispensational doctrinal clarification comes into light.

> ***With the Holy Spirit, there is always hope for change.***

Jesus, when addressing the Jews under the law, allowed divorce if the spouse was in sexual sin. This was apparently because those living under the law did not have God the Holy Spirit living in them.

But later, Paul, speaking to Believers in the Church Age, said there is zero reason for divorce, even if the spouse is in sexual sin! **Post-cross Believers have the capacity to love and forgive that those living prior to the cross didn't have.** We, post-cross, have the Holy Spirit from which to draw incredible power.

> *"I can do all things through Him who strengthens me." Phil. 4:13*

So, Christians should never get divorced. Christ living in you has the power to overcome the vilest of problems. And with the Holy Spirit, there is always hope for change. If a couple is having marriage problems, regardless of what those problems are, the answer is never divorce. Never.

"Is anything too difficult for the LORD?" Gen. 18:14a

Unfortunately however, many, many Christians have been divorced. So where do they stand? God's Word is very clear, yet many church leaders seem to ignore the instructions.

First of all, it makes no difference if both spouses were Believers or non-Believers at the time of the divorce, or if one was a Believer and one was a pagan. God's instructions to all are the same.

...it makes no difference if both spouses were Believers or non-Believers at the time of the divorce...

Sin is sin. There are no big sins and little sins. There may be ramifications in this life if you are a homosexual, or a murderer, or divorced, but nothing too large to cover with His blood. For Believers, ALL our sin was paid on the cross–past, present, and future. If you are a Believer, as far as divorce is concerned, your sin is under the blood, just like the rest of your sins. It may affect you the rest of your life, but as far as God is concerned, it's paid for and over with.

*"When you were dead in your transgressions and the uncircumcision of your flesh, He made you alive together with Him, having forgiven us **all** our transgressions, having canceled out the certificate of*

debt consisting of decrees against us, which was hostile to us; and He has taken it out of the way, having nailed it to the cross." Col. 2:13-14

There are several verses that God inspired for us to understand how to deal with specific situations. If you get divorced, regardless of the reason, the first thing God wants is for you to be reconciled to your spouse.

"...but if she does leave, let her remain unmarried, or else be reconciled to her husband." 1Cor. 7:11a

But if reconciliation is not possible, it's **best** to stay unmarried in order to fully serve the Lord.

"... to secure undistracted devotion to the Lord." 1Cor. 7:35

"But I say to the unmarried and to widows that it is good for them if they remain even as I [unmarried]." 1Cor. 7:8

"Yet such [divorced or widowed who remarry] will have trouble in this life, and I am trying to spare you." 1Cor. 7:28b

However, if two Believers fall in love, they should marry, divorced or not, and it is not sin!

*"Are you bound to a wife? Do not seek to be released. Are you released from a wife? Do not seek a wife. **But if you marry, you have not sinned;**" 1Cor. 7:27-28a*

It is interesting that the Bible says, "But if you marry, you have not sinned." That's consistent with this verse:

"But if they do not have self-control, let them marry; for it is better to marry than to burn [in lust]." 1Cor. 7:9

God created us to be married. He gave us desires for the opposite sex. But divorce is of Satan, and it horribly smashes God's model of marriage.

Therefore, if someone is divorced, the first step would be to reconcile. I'm sure a lot of people will roll their eyes over that one, but how big is your God?

But if they can't reconcile, they are to stay unmarried. And if someone is not able to stay single, which is the NORMAL case, it is much better to be married if you find a Godly spouse.

Why is the divorce percentage the same or higher for Christians than non-Christians?

Keep in mind that to God, all Believers are sanctified, cleansed, pure to the point that God can live in them, and they stay in that condition until they die or are raptured. Divorce doesn't change someone's sanctification. It's not the unpardonable sin. It was paid for on the cross just like all other sins.

Some argue that 1 Timothy 3:2 and Titus 1:6 show that there is a penalty for divorce in terms of church leadership.

> *"An overseer, then, must be above reproach, **the husband of one wife**, temperate, prudent, respectable, hospitable, able to teach," 1Tim. 3:2*

> *"...namely, if any man be above reproach, **the husband of one wife**, having children who believe, not accused of dissipation or rebellion." Titus 1:6*

This argument is not Scriptural. In the original Greek, the phrase "the husband of one wife" literally means "a one-woman man." There are many men who have been married only once who are not "one-woman men," and many who are divorced who are indeed "one-woman men." "Not divorced" is not the qualification for church Elder leadership but rather his maturity as a Believer.

The obvious exception would be if a divorce was a result of a man's poor leadership in his family, THAT would be a disqualification for church leadership. But not the divorce in itself.

> *"He must be one who manages his own household well, keeping his children under control with all dignity (but if a man does not know how to manage his own household, how will he take care of the church of God?);" 1Tim. 3:4-5*

It has often been said that God can't use someone until they've been broken. Divorce rattles people to the core and almost always brings true humility, a Christian characteristic much revered by God.

Therefore, for someone to say that a divorced man is not fit for church leadership based solely on his divorce status is prideful in itself. This is adding to God's word, being legalistic and potentially missing great leadership and input.

So all this begs the question, "Why is the divorce percentage the same or higher for Christians than non-Christians?" Well, as it turns out, the percentage changes dramatically when you ask one more question: "Do you pray daily with your spouse?"

For those couples who pray with each other daily, the percentage getting a divorce...

For those couples who pray with each other daily, the percentage getting a divorce drops from over 50% to less than 2%. So if you're committed to serving the Lord together, Agape love each other, and pray with each other daily, the odds are you're not going to get a divorce. And if you're not praying daily with your spouse, you should start!

As I mentioned, at one of our *Steeling the Mind Bible Conferences*, we had a retired divorce attorney speak. His story is amazing. Before God saved him, he drew up divorce papers for everyone who came in his office seeking a divorce. But once he trusted the shed blood of Jesus on the cross in payment for his sins, God opened his eyes to the definition of true Agape love.

After much study in God's Word, he began to see marriage and love in a different light. God had given him great insight into what God's love really is. He was burdened that most people were getting divorced because of a lack of knowledge.

So he decided to share what he learned with those coming in for a divorce. He explained to each and every couple that he would draw up the divorce papers only after a two-hour explanation of marriage and love based on the Word of God.

...drops from over 50% to less than 2%.

That two-hour pre-divorce conference resulted in seventy percent of those coming in to get back together, and they are still married today! Yes, you read that correctly! Seventy percent who went to him for a divorce are still married today! Wow!

I was so dumbfounded by that statistic that I asked him to make a scaled down one-hour presentation of his (God's) material, and the results have been absolutely phenomenal. There were five marriages that we know of that have been turned around after hearing his presentation. Some churches are now requiring **any** couple in a marriage difficulty to view this DVD prior to any counseling.

If you know anyone who is having a marriage problem, get this presentation to him or her. It'll also take a good marriage higher. The title is “How to Love Your Spouse, Regardless!” Please help us get this material out to as many as possible.

You can download and watch the video for free, or purchase the DVD to be mailed to you at **compass.org** or call 208-762-7777.

CHAPTER FIVE

SATAN'S CLAWS / SANTA'S CLAWS

A typical question we often receive in our daily devotional *Good Morning Lord!* letters to Compass is:

> *"Is there anything wrong with Christians allowing their children to think Santa Claus is real?"*

Yes, there is one really big reason not to allow your kids to believe in "Santa." But first, here are the typical answers given by Christians:

> *"Give me a break, children are usually so young when they are doing Santa that it could hardly matter!"*

> *"My parents played the Santa game and it didn't hurt me, so what's the big deal?"*

> *"When my children ask if Santa is real, then I will tell them the truth. But until they ask, I enjoy watching their little eyes light up on Christmas morning."*

A pastor with a large national following once said:

> *"I find it impossible to believe God will be eclipsed by the silhouette of Santa's sleigh rising in the Christmas sky."*

An MSNBC article said this:

> *"Fully 86 percent in the poll believed in Santa as a child. And despite the multiethnic nature of the country, more than 60 percent of those with children at home consider Santa important in their holiday celebrations now."*
> *AP-AOL News poll*

So, with so many Christians intertwining Christmas with Santa, at least when their kids are at an early age, could anything really be wrong with it?

Let's start with a simple question, "Should Christians lie?"

But as I said, there's a strong case it's VERY wrong. Here's why.

Let's start with a simple question, *"Should Christians lie?"*

God says:

> *"Truthful lips will be established forever, But a lying tongue is only for a moment." Prov. 12:19*

The Bible says we have a sinful nature:

"Transgressing and denying the LORD, And turning away from our God, Speaking oppression and revolt, Conceiving in and uttering from the heart ***lying*** *words." Isa. 59:13*

"...for ***all*** *have sinned and fall short of the glory of God," Rom. 3:23*

And the sinful nature doesn't go away when we trust Jesus' shed blood and are born again:

"For I know that nothing good dwells in me, that is, in my flesh; for the willing is present in me, but the doing of the good is not." Rom. 7:18

God says there are seven things He HATES—two of them are about lying and three of the other five could easily include lying.

There are six things which the LORD hates, Yes, seven which are an abomination to Him: Haughty eyes, a ***lying*** *tongue, And hands that shed innocent blood, A heart that devises wicked plans, Feet that run rapidly to evil, A false witness who utters* ***lies****, And one who spreads strife among brothers. Prov. 6:16-19*

Therefore, based on the Word of God, God hates lying—all lying about anything, anytime, anywhere. He hates it so much that lying will be non-existent in the New Heaven and Earth (Revelation 21:27, 22:15).

So the next question is: "Is allowing your kids to believe that "Santa" is real the same as lying to them?" Yes, it is. You can't call it anything else, no matter how innocent you think it is. All lies are from Satan and used for his purposes.

And when your kids eventually find out that you lied to them about Santa, no matter how good your intentions, you have a credibility problem when you tell them about the things of God.

Think about it...they can't see Santa, they only believe what you say about him. Neither can they see God.

Websters' definition of "lie" includes this phrase:

> *"... a situation involving deception or founded on a mistaken impression."*

So it seems pretty clear that Christians who mislead their kids about Santa are lying to them, and God calls it an "abomination."

What's even more remarkable is that the truth is so much better. What in the world is wrong with teaching our kids that Christmas is the celebration of the birth of Jesus, our Savior? It's the greatest story ever. Why go with the false when the truth is so much better?

I realize that debunking Santa in your home, especially if you have kids, is not easy. We took the "no Santa tack" as we raised our two girls. It caused several awkward moments because there were so many kids and adults into Santa Claus.

We simply taught our kids that Christmas was Jesus' birthday and Santa was a lie. We also taught them that they were sinners and needed a Savior. You can imagine what happened when well-meaning adults would come up and say, *"Is Santa coming to see you?"*

They would say emphatically, "Nooooo!" That invariably brought on the next question, "Well, have you been bad?"

And the kids would respond, shyly, "Yes."

By the time they explained their limited understanding of "He who says he has no sin deceives himself," that Santa was for non-Christians, and that they thought it was wrong to pray to the Jesus-substitute "Santa Claus," the adult was usually red-faced with embarrassment.

But the upside was that our Christmas celebrations have been, and still are, full of joy. There are gifts, and surprises, and wonderment—but it's always centered around Jesus, not a fictional character who mimics the omniscience and omnipresence of God.

Santa Claus is nothing more than a poor Jesus substitute promoting an ungodly works doctrine ("He knows if you've been bad or good ...").

Susie and I are the first to admit we made a lot of mistakes with our kids! So please don't think for a moment that we're saying "do what we do." I'm just pointing out that it can be done—by the graciousness of God—and a lot of prayer!

So our hope is that you ask the Lord to give you wisdom and confidence in this tricky area. Because Santa Claus may very well be Satan's Claws in disguise!

CHAPTER SIX

A FLOOD OF EVIDENCE

"Be diligent to present yourself approved to God as a workman who does not need to be ashamed, accurately handling the word of truth." 2Tim. 2:15

God says He inspired (God-breathed) every single word of the Bible. Peter explains it this way:

"But know this first of all, that no prophecy of Scripture is a matter of one's own interpretation, for no prophecy was ever made by an act of human will, but men moved by the Holy Spirit spoke from God." 2Pet. 1:20-21

Paul specifically mentions divine inspiration at least three times:

"For I would have you know, brethren, that the gospel which was preached by me is not according to man. For I neither received it from man, nor was I taught it, but I received it through a revelation of Jesus Christ." Gal. 1:11-12

"All Scripture is inspired by God and profitable for teaching, for reproof, for correction, for training in righteousness; so that the man of God may be adequate, equipped for every good work." 2Tim. 3:16-17

"For this reason we also constantly thank God that when you received the word of God which you heard from us, you accepted it not as the word of men, but for what it really is, the word of God, which also performs its work in you who believe." 1Thes. 2:13

Jesus tells us God's Word is accurate and dependable down to the last letter:

"For truly I say to you, until heaven and earth pass away, not the smallest letter or stroke shall pass from the Law until all is accomplished." Matt. 5:18

God is saying that the Bible is 100% inspired, 100% accurate, from beginning to end, from Genesis 1 to Revelation 22.

Therefore, we believe the Genesis 1 account of God CREATING the heavens and earth in six literal 24-hour days about 6000 years ago. He CREATED all of it out of nothing, speaking it into existence.

"For He spoke, and it was done; He commanded, and it stood fast." Psa. 33:9

> *"Praise Him, sun and moon; Praise Him, all stars of light! Praise Him, highest heavens, and the waters that are above the heavens! Let them praise the name of the LORD, for He commanded and they were created." Psa. 148:3-5*

God says that when everything was originally created it was "very good."

> *"God saw all that He had made, and behold, it was very good. And there was evening and there was morning, the sixth day." Gen. 1:31*

So earth was created as a **sinless paradise without death or decay**. Death entered the world only when the first two humans rebelled/sinned.

The theory of evolution mocks God's Word by claiming death came long before man. But the Bible is clear—first God created man, then man sinned, then death ensued.

God thankfully provided a way ultimately out of the sinful mess, but the infection of sin remained in humans forever, passed down throughout all succeeding generations.

The sin of the world got so bad in Noah's day that about 4500 years ago God flooded the entire earth with water in JUDGMENT! The earth still bears those scars today.

This judgment was necessary to wipe out the rampant ungodly sinful ways of mankind who focused on serving the creature, not the creator.

The flood of Noah destroyed the world and all life that was in it—except for what survived via Noah's Ark. It was quite a judgment!

> *"The water prevailed more and more upon the earth, so that* ***all the high mountains everywhere under the heavens were covered."*** *Gen. 7:19*

Not A Local Flood!

Despite what some yahoos are claiming, this was not a local flood. God says the entire earth was covered in water. In this judgment, millions—probably billions—of people perished, plus animals, birds and reptiles.

> ***Millions, probably billions, of people perished, plus animals, birds and reptiles.***

Peter warns us that in the last days people will mock two pillars of the Bible: 1) Jesus' rapturous return and 2) the global flood.

> *"Know this first of all, that* ***in the last days mockers*** *will come with their mocking, following after their own lusts, and saying,* ***'Where is the promise of His coming?*** *For ever since the fathers fell asleep, all continues just as it was from the beginning of creation.'*

> *For when they maintain this, it escapes their notice that by the word of God the heavens existed long ago and the earth was formed out of water and by water, through which* ***the world at that time was destroyed, being flooded with water."*** *2Pet. 3:3-6*

That's the kind of thing we at Compass spend most of our time defending—Bible prophecy and Biblical apologetics.

This chapter deals with Biblical apologetics. If God flooded the entire earth with water about 4500 years ago, killing all life except what was preserved on Noah's Ark, an event of that magnitude should have left worldwide signs we can still observe today.

An event of that magnitude should have left worldwide signs we can still observe today.

And, as expected, there ARE amazing evidences for any and all to see who wish to know the truth.

For those of us who trust God's Word, we know the water from the flood came not only from the sky but also from below the crust of the earth.

> *"...all the fountains of the great deep burst open, and the floodgates of the sky were opened." Gen. 7:11b*

This explains why we know that the sedimentary layers seen around the world were laid down by water according to weight and density (heaviest settles first, next heaviest, etc.). It also explains why the millions of the same fossils are found throughout all strata layers.

The Biblical account of Noah's flood is the simple explanation for all of this. Yet evolutionists look at the same sedimentary layers and say they were laid down over millions of years. They can't explain why the same fossils are in every layer and claim it's just a coincidence that the layers are graduated bottom to top, exactly by weight and density. They have to ignore the obvious. Both are looking at the same evidence. It's just how the evidence is *interpreted.*

On our Grand Canyon trip each year, we visit a spot where the evolutionists who manage the park have erected a geological column to explain how the sedimentary layers of the earth were formed over billions of years.

Yet, we use the same display to perfectly explain the Biblical account in the Bible. The difference is they arbitrarily add billions of years in order to maintain their old-earth beliefs. Without the magic bullet of "time," the theory of evolution falls apart.

The picture on the next page shows the secular display showing "millions of years." But using this same display, the Biblical account explains that the stone at the bottom is original creation bedrock (see #1). On top of the original creation rock, the angled layers are the layers of sediment formed from the flood (see #2). Originally these layers were laid down horizontally, but they were pushed up at an angle when God raised the mountains and lowered the valleys toward the end of Noah's flood (Psalm 104:6-9). The top layers (see #3) were deposited after the mountains were raised and the valleys were lowered, stirring up more silt, which settled by weight and density into horizontal layers.

Worldview vs. Biblical View

All around the world there are layers of sediment, laid down by water according to weight and density, containing millions of dead things, exactly what you would expect if the Biblical account were true.

Another example is the nearly vertical solid-rock walls of the Grand Canyon. On our tours we show the scientific evidences that line up with its having been formed quickly over a matter of days or weeks. Yet evolutionists look at the same information and say it happened over millions of years. Secular scientists can't explain:

- The almost vertical walls cut out of solid rock.
- The mile of missing sediment above the canyon.

- The fact that the end of the canyon is a mile higher than the beginning. Hello—the principle of gravity means water doesn't run uphill!

Science Is Always Changing

Over the years the official explanation of what carved the Grand Canyon has changed. And as more pure science is applied, it will be reexplained again and again, to defend old-earth beliefs.

Only the Bible explains the Grand Canyon scientifically. The NEVER-changing Word of God is always trustworthy over changing science.

Flood Stories

I've always found it fascinating that when Abraham was alive, one of Noah's sons, Shem, was still alive on the earth.

Abraham could very well have talked to Shem, getting a first-hand spine-tingling account of the horrific world flood. Maybe that was an additional motivating factor when Abraham "believed God" and left everything he had when God called him to leave Ur and travel to the unknown future Promised Land!

Think about it, if there was a global flood only a few thousand years ago and all the families of the world came from the survivors on Noah's ark, you would expect there to be similar stories around the earth in other cultures.

And that's what you find. Despite a language division not long after the flood (due to the Tower of Babel), some 300 to 500 different variations of the flood story have survived to this day across all seven world continents.

In fact, MOST cultures around the world have a flood legend! Many authors have documented this phenomenon: John Morris, Ken Ham, Laura Welch, Nozomi Osanai, and Bodie Hodge, just to name a few.

All document the worldwide stories of a global flood with survivors in a boat, with varying degrees of understandable differences. The number of people, the size of the boat, and the length of time on the boat may differ, but overall the stories are remarkably consistent.

...some 300 to 500 different variations of the flood story have survived to this day across all seven world continents.

In ancient Babylon, the flood story has a man building a ship to save his family and animals from a flood from a wrathful god. They end up on a mountain top.

Greek mythology has angry gods who planned to flood the earth and destroy humanity. One man takes shelter with his wife in an ark and they survive.

Even the American Indians have a flood legend where people took shelter in a boat to survive a flood. Of all the flood legends, 95% have the flood being global, 70% have people in a boat and 57% have the survivors ending up on a mountain top.

This is an incredible observable confirmation that the flood of Noah was both real and recent. If there was no global flood and the earth was millions of years old, you would expect there to be NO flood stories. There's simply no other reason hundreds of cultures worldwide have global flood stories embedded in their history.

Could the whole earth even be flooded? The Bible says that before land, before light, before anything, the earth was originally created as ALL water.

Scientists confirmed they have discovered massive volumes of water below the earth's surface.

"The earth was formless and void, and darkness was over the surface of the deep, and the Spirit of God was moving over the surface of the waters."
Gen. 1:2

"...the earth was formed out of water and by water,"
2Pet. 3:5b

Scientists are convinced that there has been flooding on Mars in the past. Some even think the entire planet was once covered in water. They think this despite the fact that not one drop of water has ever been found on Mars today.

Yet for centuries the same scientists have scoffed that the earth could have had a global flood, despite the fact it's currently 71% covered by water!

But recently scientists confirmed they have discovered massive volumes of water below the earth's surface. According to *U.S. News and World Report*, scientists now believe there is two or three times as much water below the earth's crust as currently in all the oceans between the earth's mantle and outer core.

And we already know that if we hypothetically smoothed out the earth's surface around the entire globe by leveling the mountains and filling in the oceans, the earth would be covered with water—two miles deep!

However, scientists today cannot even give the slightest chance of the possibility of a global flood because it wipes out the evolutionary theories taught as fact in secular schools... explaining the truth behind the massive amounts of fossil layers found worldwide.

> *"...always learning and never able to come to the knowledge of the truth." 2Tim. 3:7*

But for those whose faith is in the Word of God, we have truth on our side. We can boldly examine the mountains of evidence in the light of Scripture and see that the Grand Canyon is God's remarkable visual reminder of the ramifications of the last time God judged the world.

The Bible IS true, accurate, and trustworthy. God's worldwide judgment of sin using a worldwide flood did happen about 4500 years ago. And the Bible says another worldwide judgment is coming in the future. You can take that to the bank!

CHAPTER SEVEN

IS REPENTANCE NECESSARY FOR SALVATION?

The "repentance in salvation" question is hotly debated between the dispensationalists and covenant theologians. The idea of "salvation without repentance" understandably sends many into fits of rage. But is salvation without repentance even possible?

The Greek word for "repent" can be used as a noun or a verb, so it is imperative to look at the context of the verse to determine how it is being used.

The Greek word for "repent" is *metanoia* (noun) or *metanoeo* (verb). It means "to change your mind," and the context must determine what is involved in that change of mind. Does it mean repent for salvation (addressing non-Believers) or repent from error or sin (addressing Believers)?

Strong's defines the two words this way:

1. (NOUN) *metanoia*, met-an -́oy-ah; from 3340; (subjectively) compunction (for guilt, including reformation); by implication, reversal (of [another's] decision): - repentance.

2. (VERB) *metanoeo*, met-an-o-eh -́o; from 3326 and 3539; to think differently or afterwards, i.e. reconsider (morally, feel compunction): - repent.

When the word repent was used in the Gospels, speaking to the Jews under the law (e.g., Mark 1:15; Acts 3:19) who had rejected Jesus as the Messiah, the word used was the verb "*metanoeo*" ... they needed to think differently/ reconsider what they thought about who Jesus was.

But in, for instance, 2 Corinthians 7:10, a different Greek word was used, "*metanoia*." They had a "change of mind" about trusting self, good works, or tradition and instead trusted the "finished" work of Jesus on the cross.

Nowhere in the Bible are "believe" and "repent" used together to teach two different requirements for salvation.

Therefore, when salvation from the sinful state is in view, "repent" (a change of mind) and "believe" (a change of what you're trusting) are in essence used as synonyms.

In Acts 20:21 the two words, repentance and faith, are joined by one article in the Greek text which means that the two are inseparable, although each focuses on a different part of the single requirement of needing a saving faith in the Gospel.

Lewis Chafer wrote:

> *"Too often, when it is asserted—as it is here—that repentance is not to be added to belief as a separated requirement for salvation, it is assumed that repentance is not necessary to salvation. Therefore it is as dogmatically stated as language can declare, that* ***repentance is essential to salvation and that none could be saved apart from repentance, but it is included in believing and cannot be separated from it****" (Lewis Sperry Chafer, Vital Theological Issues, Roy B. Zuck, General Editor, Kregel, Grand Rapids, 1994, p. 119).*

Roy B. Zuck writes:

> *"Repentance is included in believing. Faith and repentance are like two sides of a coin.* ***Genuine faith includes repentance, and genuine repentance includes faith.*** *The Greek word for repentance (metanoia) means to change one's mind. But to change one's mind about what? About sin, about one's adequacy to save himself, about Christ as the only way of salvation, the only One who can make a person righteous" ("Kindred Spirit," a quarterly publication of Dallas Seminary, Summer 1989, p. 5).*

Luke substituted repentance in place of belief in Luke 24:46-47.

"...and He said to them, 'Thus it is written, that the Christ should suffer and rise again from the dead the third day, and that repentance for forgiveness of sins would be proclaimed in His name to all the nations, beginning from Jerusalem.'" Luke 24:46-47

Dr. Charles Ryrie says of this verse:

"Clearly, ***repentance for the forgiveness of sins is connected to the death and resurrection of Christ****" (Charles C. Ryrie, So Great Salvation, Victor Books, p. 98).*

Dr. John Ankerberg stated at a *Steeling the Mind Bible Conference*, Vail, Colorado, 1997 :

"It's not 'faith' that saves you, but rather, the 'object of your faith.' *You can have faith that your good works will save you, but they won't. The only thing that can save you is your faith and belief in the Gospel of Jesus Christ."*

The object of your faith must be the Gospel of Jesus Christ alone.

Other passages clearly support the fact that repentance often means faith in the Gospel of Jesus Christ. (Acts 10:43 with 11:17-18; Acts 13:38-39 with 2:38; and Acts 16:31 uses only "believe.")

Ryrie also points out that in some 50 uses of "faith" or "believe," the Gospel of John never uses the word repent, and bringing men to faith is the written purpose of the Book of John (John 20:31). Did John miss something? Did he give only half the gospel? If Nicodemus (John 3) needed to repent, "believe" is used interchangeably in place of "repent."

Neither did Jesus tell the woman at the well in Samaria to repent. When she recounted her story, the other Samaritans didn't "repent," rather they "believed."

> *"Belief in Christ, as an expression of a change of mind, focuses on the new direction that change about God must take, namely, trusting in Christ, God's Son, as personal Savior.* ***Jews needed to change their minds about Jesus and realize that He is their true Messiah."*** *(Charles C. Ryrie, So Great Salvation, Victor Books, p. 98).*

When we are convicted about that sin, we need to repent, or change directions, away from the sin.

And finally there is, of course, repentance needed in our Christian walk in relation to specific sins we may/will commit (2 Corinthians 7:9; Revelation 2:5).

Christians do sin, and when we are convicted about that sin, we need to repent, or change directions, away from the sin toward God's way. But this repentance has nothing to do with salvation. It's simply a Believer maturing in his/her faith.

Also, it is worth noting that both Nicodemus (John 3:2) and Joseph of Arimathea (John 19:38) were secret Believers. On the outside they appeared like all the other non-believing Jews. But on the inside they had saving faith in Jesus.

In conclusion, when non-Believers put their faith and trust in the Gospel of Jesus Christ, they have changed directions/repented of their faith in something that would not save them or changed directions/repented of their lack of faith in the only thing that can save them.

CHAPTER EIGHT

THE RUDIMENTS OF RAPTURE

"Then we who are alive and remain will be caught up together with them in the clouds to meet the Lord in the air, and so we shall always be with the Lord."
1Thes. 4:17

The upcoming Rapture, literally the "catching away," is to me the most intriguing of all Biblical doctrine.

Nothing could be more exciting than thinking about not dying physically but rather changing from earth to heaven in the blink of an eye. One moment everything seems normal, then instantaneously everything changes forever.

The Greek word for the term "caught up" is ***harpazo***, which means "to seize, catch up, snatch away by force."

This is the same Greek word used to describe how the Spirit "snatched" Philip away from the Ethiopian eunuch.

"When they came up out of the water, the Spirit of the Lord snatched (Greek - "harpazo") Philip away; and the eunuch no longer saw him, but went on his way rejoicing. But Philip found himself at Azotus," Acts 8:39-40a

Philip was miraculously transported by God, in the blink of an eye, from one place to another. (Imagine him telling that story to his family!)

The English word "rapture" comes from a Latin word, *rapio*, which means to seize or snatch in relation to being carried away in spirit or in body from one place to another. Therefore, the Rapture of the church is the forceful removal, or carrying away, of Believers from earth to heaven. The purpose of the Rapture is to remove the Believers on earth before the Tribulation with God's judgmental wrath begins.

Most Believers living today sense the day of the Rapture is getting close. I think the current generations have an odds-on chance of being in this ultimately famous group if they live out a normal lifespan.

We easily see that what was written prophetically about the end of the Church Age is happening all around us! How close we are to our exodus we don't really know. But most solid Bible scholars sense the end of this age could be quite close.

Just living in this time period is tough. We recoil when we see perversion flaunted as normal. We cringe when we see sin exalted. And we know the Lord ranks lying up there in the same category as murder. Yet it's commonplace and mostly unchallenged in our nation today.

> *"Woe to those who enact evil statutes and to those who constantly record unjust decisions" Is. 10:1*

> ***The Rapture of the church is the forceful removal, or carrying away, of Believers from earth.***

God Gave Us Prophecy for Comfort

We know the Bible warns of God's coming judgment on sin, but at the same time we're COMFORTED by what we know about Bible prophecy! After discussing the Rapture of Believers, Paul ends with this sentence:

> *"Therefore **comfort** one another with these words" 1Thes. 4:18.*

God's promise of the Rapture is comforting because it's His promise and assurance we'll NOT be part of the earth's horrific seven-year tribulation, God's horrific, worldwide judgment on sinful mankind.

God's Purpose for Rapture

Therefore, the purpose of the Rapture is to bring to an end the dispensation of the Church Age and remove Believers before God's undiluted wrath comes upon earth.

"For God has not destined us for wrath, but for obtaining salvation through our Lord Jesus Christ," *1Thes. 5:9*

There is also a practical side necessitating the Rapture. Jesus explained to His disciples that God's Holy Spirit could not come to earth to indwell Believers until He first departed earth.

"But I tell you the truth, it is to your advantage that I go away; for if I do not go away, the Helper will not come to you; but if I go, I will send Him to you." John 16:7

Jesus departed earth, enabling the Holy Spirit to come to earth, permanently indwelling all Believers (Acts 2).

Therefore, now the reverse is necessary. God's Spirit must be removed in order for Jesus to return. When God removes His Spirit, all who have His Spirit are swept away at the same time..."caught up."

The Bible records others being "caught up" to heaven in the past. So we can get a glimpse of what will transpire at that spine-tingling moment.

Enoch Was Raptured

The first to be raptured, or "taken up" to heaven before death, was Enoch, who lived prior to Abraham.

> *"Enoch walked with God; and he was not, for God took him." Gen. 5:24*

> *"By faith **Enoch was taken up so that he would not see death;** AND HE WAS NOT FOUND BECAUSE GOD TOOK HIM UP; for he obtained the witness that before his being taken up he was pleasing to God." Heb. 11:5*

Paul Was Raptured

Paul was also raptured, or "caught up" to heaven, when he was living on the earth.

> *"I know a man in Christ who fourteen years ago—whether in the body I do not know, or out of the body I do not know, God knows—such a man was **caught up to the third heaven.**" 2Cor. 12:2*

This "catching away" to heaven left a lasting impression on Paul. So profound was the experience that the Lord had to give him a "thorn in the flesh" to keep him humble back here on earth.

> *"Because of the surpassing greatness of the revelations [seeing heaven], for this reason, to keep me from exalting myself, there was given me a thorn in the flesh,*

a messenger of Satan to torment me—to keep me from exalting myself!" 2Cor. 12:7

God also forbade Paul from talking about what he saw in heaven, a fact that makes me heavily discount ANYTHING someone says about dying, going to heaven, and coming back.

"...was caught up into Paradise and heard inexpressible words, which a man is not permitted to speak." 2Cor. 12:4

The "Great Lie" in the Tribulation

Undoubtedly, there will have to be an explanation to those left behind as to what happened to all the missing people. The Bible calls it the "Lie."

"For this reason God will send upon them a deluding influence (Greek = "activity of error") so that they will believe what is false, (THE LIE)" 2Thes. 2:11

It's quite possible that The Great Lie will be the explanation of what happened to all of the Believers who suddenly disappeared. Millions will vanish without warning and without a trace of where they went.

Tim LaHaye surmises that all the clothes of the raptured people will be left in a pile from where they were sitting/standing/lying. That seems logical since you won't need your clothes in heaven.

But Ed Hindson says if that's what happens at the Rapture, then what about people who wear glasses? You would assume, then, glasses would be left behind. If so, then what about braces, false teeth, and fillings? Surely they would be left behind too. Taking that train of thought, you get to transplanted limbs, hair, and organs that are not your own...would they be left behind?

What about fake hips, knees, and breasts? The list is endless. Ed Hindson surmises that some might have more left behind than taken up! It's an interesting thought.

Regardless, the sudden disappearance of so many will cause massive disruptions. Cars wrecking and planes falling due to drivers and pilots who vanished are only the tip of the iceberg. Key business leaders, prison guards, and born-again pastors will be gone. And possibly even key politicians might be missing.

Therefore, "The Lie" could be that people from another planet or universe removed those who were ruining the planet. Or they were taken to another planet for reprogramming. That would also explain the 50-year push to make UFOs plausible.

Or "The Lie" could refer to the middle of the Tribulation when Satan is cast to earth. It's at this time the devil indwells the body of the three-days-dead world leader, bringing him back to life and claiming to be the resurrected Messiah... thus becoming the False Messiah/ Abomination of Desolation (Daniel 11:31 / Matthew 24:15).

Blessings from Studying the Rapture

Lastly, the fact you're interested in reading this chapter, looking forward to meeting Jesus in the air at the Rapture, puts you in a special category of people: those LOOKING for that incredible day to arrive.

> *"...in the future there is laid up for me the **crown of righteousness**, which the Lord, the righteous Judge, will award to me on that day; and not only to me, but also to all **who have loved His appearing**." 2Tim. 4:8*

Also, the Book of Revelation, which contains almost all prophecy, is the only book in the Bible promising a blessing for just reading it!

> *"Blessed is he who reads and those who hear the words of the prophecy..." Rev. 1:3*

So, you're blessed for looking forward to the Rapture. You're blessed to be excluded from receiving God's wrath in the Tribulation. And you're also blessed/comforted by the fact God is still in control! And throughout it all, when we die or are raptured, we win! Gotta love that!

We should pray always that the Lord will give us more and more occasions to explain what we know.

> *"Conduct yourselves with wisdom toward outsiders, making the most of the opportunity." Col. 4:5*

> *"...he who turns a sinner from the error of his way [allows the Lord to use him/her] will save his soul from death and will cover a multitude of sins."* James 5:20

Think about it. We've been studying the Bible all our lives in order to be able to respond to all this—and now is the time to put to practical use what we've learned!

The bottom line is that we're most likely living in the last of the last days, a special generation of Believers who can be like Noah, testifying about Biblical truth right up to the end!

Millions Missing?

If, in the blink of an eye, a large number of people all over the earth have mysteriously vanished into thin air, go to this link to find out what really happened!

compass.org/mm

CHAPTER NINE

KILLERS IN THE KITCHEN!

"Satan is the god of this world." 2Cor. 4:4

"Satan is the father of lies." John 8:44

"We are aliens on this planet." 1Pet. 2:11

If Satan is the god of this world and the father of lies, then it's not a stretch to think that all the people on the earth are being lied to in one form or another all the time. The only thing we can trust is the Bible.

So as Believers we look to the Lord to meet our needs. He is our sustainer. But we still have to live as aliens on a planet full of lies, waiting for God to redeem the earth from Satan's control.

And as we move closer to the Rapture, we can easily see many of the end-time events beginning to line up. For instance, people of earth are looking more and more to governments, rather than to God, to meet their basic needs. The ultimate goal of Satan is to move everyone toward a one-world government.

Can Government Meet our Basic Needs?

The problems arising from kicking God out of government are growing exponentially. If I could use only one word to describe them all, it would be "lies."

Let's face it, if you're not seeking God, you ARE seeking Satan, who is "a liar and the father of lies." (John 8:44) It's gotten to the point no one trusts any government official because they're all liars!

And just when you thought it couldn't get any worse, it has. It's not just the IRS and State Department that have been lying to us. The Food and Drug Administration (FDA) is just as guilty. For decades, they have allowed poison into the food supply. Yes, poison!

That's an incredible statement to make, but our grocery store FOOD is killing us! And they work hard to hide this truth.

Apparently there are a LOT of people who already know the problems with the food we consume daily. I admit I've been asleep at the wheel regarding this subject and am just now taking the time to look into it. But with very little research, the facts are shocking to say the least.

And I must apologize for rolling my eyes every time somebody would try to tell me things not to eat. I just couldn't believe our food delivery system was that unhealthy. But it is... it's atrocious.

Overweight America

Gallup tells us that two thirds of Americans are overweight. Duh. Look around. Seems higher than that. But is all that extra weight due to "lack of exercise" and "poor diet?" I will show you facts that say "no."

Diabetes is skyrocketing— 20 million Americans have diabetes, and another 57 million have pre-diabetes. What happened in the '70s, '80s, and '90s that caused diabetes cases to escalate? Read on.

Today 77 million Americans have diabetes or pre-diabetes!

Another huge consequence of eating food on the "approved" list is heart disease. Some 75 million Americans have heart disease, and the numbers continue to climb, despite millions on diets or drugs that lower cholesterol.

Heart disease is the leading cause of death for both men and women—600,000 people will die of heart disease this year, one out of every four who die. More people will die of heart disease this year than all other causes combined!

New research is showing that the major factors contributing to America's weight gain, heart disease, and diabetes are:

1) Chemicals that the FDA has approved to be injected into animals we eat.

2) Chemicals approved to be added to the foods we consume.

3) Genetically modified (GMO) plants that both our animals eat or we directly consume.

You won't hear this on the news. Or from the government. But what you are about to read is true.

Fact: Over 70% of the antibiotics used in this country are used in animal food production.

Fact: Over 70% of the antibiotics used in this country are used in animal food production. And what's in the animals we eat affects each and every one of us.

Many, and some argue most, of today's health problems like autoimmune disorders, food reactions, Alzheimer's, and heart problems begin in our gastrointestinal tract (GI)—stomach, intestines, and all digestive organs.

If our GI can't digest foods or the chemicals added to processed foods, it becomes inflamed and our immune system doesn't function properly. And therefore we are more likely to get sick, develop allergies, become resistant to antibiotics, etc.

And for the last 50 years or so, our GI has been getting more than it can handle! Hence the problems.

Dr. Dwight Lundell, who performed over 5,000 open-heart surgeries, threw the medical community on its head by releasing a letter of apology recently. In his letter he stated, contrary to supposedly scientific opinion, that cholesterol is not the problem in heart disease.

Dr. Lundell explained that it's the inflammation in the walls of the blood vessels that causes the cholesterol to accumulate.

> *"I saw it in over 5,000 surgical patients spanning 25 years who all shared one common denominator—inflammation in their arteries."* Dr. Dwight Lundell

He goes on to state in no uncertain terms that for decades we've been treating the symptoms and not the problem. The problem is caused by the chemicals and altered/modified DNA (referred to as GMO) in the foods we're eating, not high-fat diets. In fact, the low-fat diets CONTRIBUTE to the inflammation! [https://www.sott.net/article/242516-Heart-surgeon-speaks-out-on-what-really-causes-heart-disease]

Inflammation is your body's natural defense to unnatural substances like bacteria, toxins, or viruses. As we continue to pummel our bodies with foreign chemicals that we can't process, inflammation is generated, causing cholesterol to accumulate in our arteries. The result is high blood pressure, diabetes, obesity, stroke, and heart disease.

So again, the problem is not cholesterol but rather the foods we eat that damage the walls and cell lining of our arteries. These chemicals also affect the delicate balance of natural and God-given good bacteria in our stomach and intestines that aid in digestion and work against infection.

Some 85% to 90% of corn grown in the United States is GMO.

The heart-breaker is that 60 countries ban GMO foods we digest daily. In 1988, at a scientific conference called "The International Federation of Organic Agriculture," they released this statement about GMO foods: "There are unacceptable risks involved: threats to human health, a negative and irreversible environmental impact, incompatibility with sustainable agriculture, and a violation of rights for both farmers and consumers."

In Europe, GMO food products must be labeled, but not here in America. Below are some reasons other countries have banned foods that we're eating.

Corn

In a nutshell, don't eat it. It is estimated that some 85% to 90% of corn grown in the United States is GMO—it has been genetically modified (which is basically changing its DNA) so that it can withstand massive chemical spraying.

Known as "NK603 Roundup-resistant," farmers can spray gargantuan amounts of toxic vegetation killer and only the corn survives.

There is another corn Monsanto distributes called "Bt." It has been genetically modified so that when insects eat the corn, it kills them. Let me repeat. When insects eat the corn, it kills the insects!

That means we're eating pesticide poison when we eat that corn. And the Center for Disease Control (CDC) and Environmental Protection Agency (EPA) admit pesticide is a carcinogen (cancer-causing agent).

Sherbrooke University Hospital in Quebec did a study that found the Bt toxin was detected in the blood of 93% of pregnant women, 80% of babies, and 67% of non-pregnant women.

Obviously, tinkering with God's DNA design has its downside. Bt has been toxic to humans and mammals since 1996 when it was introduced, and there has been a corresponding rise in birth defects and disorders. A study in Italy where mice were fed Bt corn showed many problems as it adversely affected their immune systems.

The mice also had an increase in interleukin cytokines, which are associated with allergies, inflammations, and even cancer. If you suffer from arthritis, MS, or cancer, you have elevated interleukins. It doesn't take a rocket scientist to see the connection.

It's safe to assume that if you're eating corn, you're probably eating GMO corn and the poison in it. And, as I mentioned, the FDA and EPA admit that most herbicides, weed killers, and insecticides are cancer-causing.

A study done in France is shocking. The corn caused premature death and up to 300% increase in tumors and liver and kidney damage of the rats. This is the same corn that comes in your corn-based breakfast cereal, tortillas, and corn snack chips.

The French study was done over a two-year period. When the scary results were tallied and made known, Monsanto, who sells both the corn seed and vegetation killers, did its own in-house study (but only three months long) trying to mitigate the revenue damage. [http://www.ijbs.com/v05p0706.htm]

Seventy percent of all processed food contains corn. This has become such a problem (as the word is getting out about problems linked to corn) for manufacturers that they have become pretty good at deceiving you into thinking that corn is not in a product when it is. [http://www.livecornfree.com/2010/04/ingredients-derived-from-corn-what-to.html]

The ingredients listed on a package may not say "corn" but rather say "citric acid." Citric acid can be, and usually is, made from corn. Other words substituted for corn are ascorbic acid, baking powder (corn starch), cellulose, dextrose, and starch. Even Morton adds dextrose to their salt!

Wheat

GMO wheat is being tested, but thankfully it's not been approved by the FDA. Red flags issued by scores of top scientists are screaming that it leads to liver failure. Hopefully the FDA won't approve GMO wheat. But unfortunately the wheat we already eat is a problem.

Back in the 1960s and 1970s, scientists began selectively breeding wheat in order for it to withstand drought, cold climates, and insect damage, thereby increasing crop yields.

The modifications also made all wheat mature at a lower height, making harvesting much easier. The result is that today's wheat has little resemblance to wheat grown 100 years ago.

Tests have shown that the "gluten" problem can be traced to wheat consumption.

Tests have shown that the "gluten" problem can be traced to wheat consumption. Digestive diseases, obesity, diabetes, heart disease, arthritis, osteoporosis, lupus, infertility, and dementia all can be traced to the modified wheat we consume daily.

I avoid wheat products in the United States as best I can because when I eat it, it makes the knuckles on my hands painfully sore. But when we're in Europe or the Middle East (Susie and I have traveled to Europe and the Middle East some 60 times) I can eat all the bread I want and my hands are unaffected. Not surprisingly I found out that the EU and Middle Eastern nations prohibit importing wheat from the United States.

Several studies have shown a direct link between autoimmune thyroid disease and gluten intolerance. Some studies suggest as many as one out of every three people are gluten intolerant! Worse, 8 in 10 people are genetically predisposed to gluten intolerance.

White bread and whole wheat bread increase blood glucose more than pure sugar. When insulin and blood sugar levels rise and fall rapidly, it makes humans more hungry...so we eat more and gain more weight. Most people will lose weight when they go on a wheat-free diet.

Milk

Most cows are fed corn. So both the milk and meat from corn-fed cattle contain poison if they're eating GMO corn.

Bovine Growth Hormone (rBGH) is a genetically modified synthetic hormone that is repeatedly injected into cows to increase milk production. At least a third of all dairy cows are injected with this GMO hormone, which is a combination of cow DNA and bacteria.

Monsanto lists on its rBGH warning label some 20 adverse effects for cows, including increase of bacterial infections, reproductive problems, milk quality problems, and increase of pus in the milk! Good grief!

Because of these problems, all 26 countries in the European Union, as well as Canada, Australia, New Zealand, Israel, and Japan have banned the use of rBGH. But not the United States.

The antibiotics used to fight the pus show up in the milk and enter humans. When we drink milk with antibiotics in it, our bodies become resistant to them, making it harder to fight infections.

But the biggest problem is that using rBGH increases "insulin-like growth factor-1" (IGBF1) in humans. When rBGH increases, the chance of breast, colon, prostate, and lung cancer as well as abnormal cell growth increase.

The FDA does NOT require labeling milk with these facts! And Monsanto has sued companies that HAVE labeled their milk as "rBGH free." This gives you a hint as to how strong the dairy lobby is in the U.S.

Aspartame

In a nutshell, this stuff is poison. If you're eating or drinking anything with Nutrasweet or Equal in it, you're eating/drinking poison.

Aspartame is in over 6,000 products consumed daily, and I guarantee you it's in products you never thought about—including most breakfast foods. And it's worse for kids as their natural defenses against the ingredients in aspartame are not fully developed.

It should never have been approved. The story of its approval sounds impossible as the FDA listed 92 symptoms caused by the poison. This is why the FDA kept it away from consumers for 15 years.

You might think I'm getting a little carried away calling it poison, but up until it was approved for human consumption, the Department of Defense was considering using it for biological warfare because it contained so much neurotoxin.

Arthur Evangelista, a former FDA Investigator, has written extensively about the problems with aspartame. [https://rense.com//general37/ddly.htm]

He outlines the role politics played in the way it was approved and that those who did illegally push it through the approval process left the FDA and took cushy jobs with the pharmaceutical companies that benefited most from the approval.

Evangelista states,

> *"**Aspartame should never have been approved.** It is neurotoxic. Its components easily transcend the blood-brain barrier, interfering with normal nerve cell function. This affects the glutathione and calcium mechanisms in place, destroying nerve cell integrity."*

> *"The methanol then breaks down into formaldehyde-formic acid components, which denaturizes/mutates*

the DNA: a known scientific fact. ***The subsequent result from this interaction and from isolates of genetically modified amino acids, the methanol, is nerve cell necrosis and subsequent organ system degradation."***

"The hypothalamus alone (the major controller for much of the endocrine system), is at especially high risk to these effects...thereby, affecting many other organ systems.

"I have seen first hand the effects on symptoms when individuals have abstained from ingesting the artificial sweetener, aspartame. Make no bones about it, aspartame is a major factor in many symptomologies due to its effects upon brain chemistry."

The amount of clinical and scientific evidence against using Aspartame is staggering. Aspartame now accounts for over 75% of the adverse reactions to food additives reported to the FDA.

Scientific studies have shown aspartame links to birth defects, brain cancer, seizures, and diabetes. Here is a partial list of other problems found:

- Headaches
- Migraines
- Dizziness
- Seizures

- Nausea
- Numbness
- Muscle spasms
- Weight gain
- Rashes
- Depression
- Fatigue
- Irritability
- Tachycardia
- Insomnia
- Vision problems
- Hearing loss
- Heart palpitations
- Breathing difficulties
- Anxiety attacks
- Slurred speech
- Loss of taste
- Tinnitus
- Vertigo
- Memory loss
- Joint pain

And research now shows that the following chronic illnesses can be triggered or worsened by consuming even small amounts of Aspartame:

- Brain tumors
- Multiple sclerosis
- Epilepsy
- Chronic fatigue syndrome
- Parkinson's disease

- Alzheimer's
- Mental retardation
- Lymphoma
- Birth defects
- Fibromyalgia
- Diabetes

In summary, when you consume Aspartame, it begins to destroy the neurons in your brain. It can destroy over half of your neurons before symptoms are seen. This type of damage has been linked to:

- Multiple sclerosis (MS)
- Parkinson's disease (ALS)
- Hypoglycemia
- Memory loss
- AIDS
- Hormonal problems
- Dementia
- Epilepsy
- Brain lesions
- Alzheimer's disease
- Neuroendocrine disorders

So I think it's safe to call this poison. It should never have been approved, and no one in their right mind should be consuming even small amounts.

BHA and BHT

Butylated hydroxyanisole (BHA) and butylated hydroxytoluene (BHT) are widely used preservatives (gum, cereal, nut mixes) that prevent oils in food from become rancid. It's known to cause cancer in rats... according to our own U.S. Department of Health and Human Services (HHS).

BHA is suspected of causing allergies and hyperactivity in children. It's banned from infants' foods in the UK, Japan, and all 16 countries of the European Union, but not in the United States.

Olestra/Olean

This fat substitute (think "Fat Free") was in potato chips that were fed to rats in a study by Purdue University. The rats GAINED WEIGHT and had problems with diarrhea and bowels.

Known to inhibit the absorption of fat soluble vitamins, the FDA requires vitamins A, D, E, and K to be added to any product made with Olean or Olestra to make up for the loss it causes! Olestra and Olean are banned in the EU and Canada.

Potassium Bromate

This is added to the bread, already made with the GMO wheat, to hold the dough together. The International Agency for Research on Cancer classifies potassium bromate as a **cancer-causing agent**. Studies have linked it to cancerous tumors, kidney damage, and thyroid tumors.

It's banned in Canada, China, and all 16 countries of the European Union, but not in the United States.

Arsenic

Seems hard to believe, but arsenic (poison) is added to over 90% of poultry to increase its weight while reducing the amount of food needed to keep the chicks alive.

Under the guise of treating parasites, it's massively pumped into poultry. And the net result is that we eat the arsenic, a known carcinogen! Arsenic in food is banned in the 16 countries of the European Union, but not in the United States.

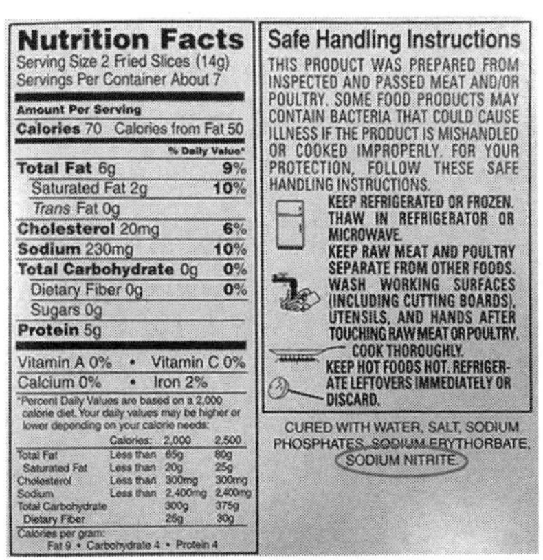

Red Meat with Sodium Nitrate

We've been hearing for years that red meat was bad for you. That is a bit of a theological problem since the Bible tells us that it's OK to eat red meat, even commanded in the Old Testament for festivals like Passover.

So what's the answer? It turns out that it's not the meat that is bad for you, but rather it's what goes into a lot of meat that's awful!

Sodium nitrate is not in chicken or fish but is added to red meat to produce that amazing red color, to preserve it until it can be sold, and to control bacterial growth.

But the dirty little secret is that **sodium nitrate causes cancer**, according to the World Cancer Research Fund. It's basically unfit for human consumption because it's linked directly to the worst of all cancers, pancreatic cancer.

In the 1970s the USDA tried to ban sodium nitrate only to be inundated with the clever "They're trying to ban bacon!" campaign launched by the meat packaging industry. Most processed meats, like packaged ham, bacon, sausage, hot dogs, pepperoni, salami, and virtually all red meat used in frozen prepared meals like pizza have sodium nitrate in them.

A study by the University of Hawaii found that eating processed meats increases the risk of pancreatic cancer by 67%! Bottom line, if you're eating sodium nitrate in meat, it's like saying "I don't care if I get cancer."

More GMO Related Problems

GMO foods are causing all kind of problems in addition to human health. They're creating superbugs and superweeds because only the strongest survive and they become resistant to insecticide. Each year more and more chemical spraying is necessary.

Bee and butterfly populations are being decimated. Pollination of crops is vital for about 40% of our food supply. Farmers in California are having to import bees to get the job done as the bee populations are not replenishing themselves as they have for the last century.

GMO seeds are the patented property of large multinational corporations like Monsanto. Farmers are forbidden to use seeds from the GMO crops already purchased and therefore are forced to buy new seeds each year, reducing the profitability of each farming operation.

Also, seeds are easily blown from farm to farm. If a farmer's crops are unintentionally cross-pollinated with the GMO-patented seeds, the farmer is criminally liable to pay royalties and licensing fees. Monsanto actually sued a farmer and won even though the farmer didn't intentionally use Monsanto seed.

Suicide Rates

This one's a heart breaker. Monsanto was able to get farmers in India to begin using their GMO seeds by promising increased crop yields.

Although the program was successful for the first five years, now it is no better than the former non-GMO crop. And it costs a lot more to operate as they have to pay more and more for pesticides to kill the superbugs.

The farmers are now losing so much money they're committing suicide by the droves—125,000 since the introduction of the GMO seeds. As a result, India's Supreme Court recommended a 10-year moratorium on using the GMO seeds so stricter regulations could be implemented.

So it seems our food supply is a mess. But trying to unplug from the traditional food supply system is a daunting task. You'll find yourself looking for local farmers and making friends at the local organic food store.

What to do-

- Always read ingredient labels. Take the time to look closely at each item you buy.
- Try to buy organic foods if you have a choice, but note that "Organic" means 80% or higher is natural. "Certified Organic" is 100% natural but is really hard to find.
- Don't buy anything made with sodium nitrite, aspertame or monosodium glutamate.
- Don't eat processed meats served by restaurants, schools, hospitals, hotels or other institutions.
- Eat more wild-caught fish (not farmed raised!) and fresh produce at meals.
- Eat more fruit and berries with antioxidants that fight against cancer-causing agents.
- Try to eliminate all corn and corn products.
- Don't eat processed foods unless you're starving to death.
- Take the time to do your own research. Much is available via the web.

It's pretty much impossible to rid 100% of the poisons from your diet. But if you can cut out 80% to 90%, you'll be far healthier.

And finally, let's keep everything in its proper perspective. The last thing we would want is for people to live longer, healthier lives and then split the gates of hell wide open.

The purpose of living healthier is to be able to be a better witness about what God CREATED. We get into trouble when the government ditches God and starts making decisions irrespective of Biblical commands.

But as we see in the book of Jonah, it's possible to repent as a nation and be given a reprieve from what we deserve.

Judgment in Nineveh was delayed 100 years or so when people turned back to the Lord. For that we pray.

Biblical Food

Our original title of this chapter was going to be "Behold a Black Horse." But after doing the research on problems with our food supply and how/why food would become so scarce in the Tribulation, I changed the title to ***Killers in the Kitchen***, as I found our current food-growing and production methods were, to say the least, shocking!

Trying to actually use this information about what to eat is hard. I don't know about you, but trying to buy food without GMO poisons seems to be next to impossible. We now shop for food much differently, mainly spending more time reading labels and groaning.

Turns out that GMO corn (poison) is in just about everything. I think half of the items in our grocery stores have some form of GMO corn in them. So we're now finding we have a lot fewer choices for breakfast, lunch, and dinner... and paying a lot more for what we do purchase in the gluten-free section or local health food store.

We know from Scripture that Jesus ate broiled fish (obviously wild-caught). We know John the Baptist ate locusts and honey. I'll skip the locusts, thank you!

Jesus drank fermented wine. I have to add "fermented" because so many Christians have been taught He drank grape juice. Not true. Grape juice came about only in the late 1800s when Pastor Welch found a way to keep grapes from naturally fermenting so he could serve non-alcoholic wine for communion.

1 Timothy 5:23 says, "*Drink a little wine for your stomach's sake,*" so we encourage those who travel with us to the Holyland to drink a "little" wine at dinner each evening.

It apparently works wonders in your digestive tract for things your body is not used to. Makes for more interesting conversation, too.

We know Jesus ate lamb, bread, figs, nuts, roasted eggs, unleavened bread, and olive oil at His Passover meals. He would have also eaten most, if not all, of the food in the list below.

Bible Foods List

A list of different foods mentioned in the Bible and sample verses:

Almonds *(Genesis 43:11; Numbers 17:8)*
Apples *(Song of Solomon 2:5)*
Barley *(Deuteronomy 8:8; Ezekiel 4:9)*
Beans *(2 Samuel 17:28; Ezekiel 4:9)*
Bread *(Genesis 25:34; 2 Samuel 6:19; 16:1; Mark 8:14)*
Butter *(Proverbs 30:33)*
Calf *(Proverbs 15:17; Luke 15:23)*
Cheese *(2 Samuel 17:29; Job 10:10)*
Cucumbers *(Numbers 11:5)*

Curds *(Isaiah 7:15)*
Dates *(2 Samuel 6:19; 1 Chronicles 16:3)*
Dove *(Leviticus 12:8)*
Eggs *(Job 6:6; Luke 11:12)*
Figs *(Numbers 13:15; Jeremiah 24:1-3)*
Fish *(Matthew 15:36; John 21:11-13)*
Flour *(2 Samuel 17:28; 1 Kings 17:12)*
Goat *(Genesis 27:9)*
Gourds *(2 Kings 4:39)*
Grapes *(Leviticus 19:10; Deuteronomy 23:24)*
Honey *(Exodus 33:3; Deuteronomy 8:8; Judges 14:8-9)*
Lamb *(2 Samuel 12:4)*
Leeks *(Numbers 11:5)*
Lentils *(Genesis 25:34; 2 Samuel 17:28; Ezekiel 4:9)*
Locust *(Mark 1:6)*
Melons *(Numbers 11:5; Isaiah 1:8)*
Milk *(Exodus 33:3; Job 10:10; Judges 5:25)*
Millet *(Ezekiel 4:9)*
Olive *(Isaiah 17:6; Micah 6:15)*
Olive Oil *(Ezra 6:9; Deuteronomy 8:8)*
Onions *(Numbers 11:5)*
Oxen *(1 Kings 19:21)*
Partridge *(1 Samuel 26:20; Jeremiah 17:11)*
Pigeon *(Genesis 15:9; Leviticus 12:8)*
Pistachio Nuts *(Genesis 43:11)*
Pomegranates *(Numbers 20:5; Deuteronomy 8:8)*
Quail *(Psalm 105:40)*
Raisins *(Numbers 6:3; 2 Samuel 6:19)*
Sheep *(Deuteronomy 14:4)*
Spelt *(Ezekiel 4:9)*
Sycamore Fruit *(Psalm 78:47; Amos 7:14)*

Unleavened Bread *(Genesis 19:3; Exodus 12:20)*
Venison *(Genesis 27:7)*
Vinegar *(Ruth 2:14; John 19:29)*
Wheat *(Ezra 6:9; Deuteronomy 8:8; Matthew 12:1)*
Wine *(Ezra 6:9; John 2:1-10)*

Spices

Coriander *(Exodus 16:31; Numbers 11:7)*
Cinnamon *(Exodus 30:23; Revelation 18:13)*
Cumin *(Isaiah 28:25; Matthew 23:23)*
Dill *(Matthew 23:23)*
Garlic *(Numbers 11:5)*
Mint *(Matthew 23:23; Luke 11:42)*
Mustard *(Matthew 13:31)*
Rue *(Luke 11:42)*
Salt *(Ezra 6:9; Job 6:6)*

References:

http://www.sott.net/article/242516-Heart-surgeon-speaks-out-on-what-really-causes-heart-disease

http://www.livecornfree.com/2010/04/ingredients-derived-from-corn-what-to.html

http://celiacdisease.about.com/od/celiacdiseasefaqs/f/Genetically-Modified-Wheat.htm

http://www.naturalnews.com/011148.html

http://chriskresser.com/the-gluten-thyroid-connection

CHAPTER TEN

IS RETIREMENT BIBLICAL?

> *"But realize this, that in the last days difficult times will come. For men will be lovers of self, lovers of money..." 2Tim. 3:1-2*

Nowhere in the Bible does it suggest that when you reach a certain age you should have enough money to sit back and do nothing. In fact, man's penalty for sin in the Garden of Eden is lifelong work.

> *"Then to Adam He said: 'Because you have listened to the voice of your wife, and have eaten from the tree about which I commanded you, saying, "You shall not eat from it;" cursed is the ground because of you; In toil you will eat of it* ***all the days of your life.****'" Gen. 3:17*

When the Israelites were wandering in the desert, God forbade them from picking up the divinely supplied manna for even one additional day except for the Sabbath. And if they did gather more than a day's worth, it spoiled.

"Then the LORD said to Moses, 'Behold, I will rain bread from heaven for you; and the people shall go out and gather a day's portion every day ... On the sixth day...it will be twice as much as they gather daily.'" Ex. 16:4-5

The world apparently believes people should be obsessed with how much they have in their "retirement account."

Yet, literally every day on television, radio, and the Internet, the number of ads proclaiming how to reach your retirement goals is mind-numbing. The world apparently believes people should be obsessed with how much they have in their "retirement account" and how much more is needed.

Commercial after commercial is highly suggestive that success in this life is all about having enough money to do what you want when you get old.

But like a lot of other things where the world's thinking is not Biblically oriented, it has the wrong long-term focus. And if we're not careful, we'll get sucked into the world's focus and away from God's truth.

The Bible is clear that this life is not about how much we accumulate in this life.

"Then He said to them, 'Beware, and be on your guard against every form of greed; for not even when one has

> *an abundance does his life consist of his possessions.'"*
> *Luke 12:15*

After making that statement, Jesus went on to tell the parable about the man who had so much he decided to build bigger barns.

> *"...'Soul, you have many goods laid up for many years to come; take your ease, eat, drink and be merry.' But God said to him, 'You fool! This very night your soul is required of you; and now who will own what you have prepared?' So is the man who stores up treasure for himself, and is not rich toward God." Luke 12:19-21*

The idea is that in this life we need to be mainly concerned with eternal things, not temporal things. Money is temporal. God is forever. Our life should be focused on eternity, not on this life.

> *"Set your mind on the things above, not on the things that are on earth." Col.3:2*

And when you have the correct long-term priorities, this life will take care of itself.

> *"[S]toring up for themselves the treasure of a good foundation for the future, so that they may take hold of that which is life indeed." 1Tim. 6:19*

This, of course, does not mean saving money is wrong. We're to be good stewards of what God has given us and that would include saving for unexpected events. The Bible says it's smart to save and even to have money left over when you die.

> *"A good man leaves an inheritance to his children's children," Prov. 13:22a*

Yet, not everyone will have an abundance. God chooses some to have more and some to have less material wealth.

> *"It is the blessing of the LORD that makes rich, And He adds no sorrow to it." Prov. 10:22*

Men are simply to work hard to provide for their families.

> *"...if anyone is not willing to work, then he is not to eat, either. For we hear that some among you are leading an undisciplined life, doing no work at all..." 2Thes. 3:10*

> *"But if anyone does not provide for his own, and especially for those of his household, he has denied the faith and is worse than an unbeliever." 1Tim. 5:8*

> *"I have been young and now I am old, Yet I have not seen the righteous forsaken or his descendants begging bread." Psa. 37:25*

When men work, they are to assume they are working for the Lord, that He is their ultimate taskmaster. They're not only to work hard but also to look at their employer or business as God-ordained, leaving the ultimate success up to the Lord.

> *"Whatever you do, do your work heartily, as for the Lord rather than for men, knowing that from the Lord you will receive the reward of the inheritance. It is the Lord Christ whom you serve." Col. 3:23-24*

> *"May the LORD give you increase, You and your children." Psa. 115:14*

This must, of course, be balanced with the fact that if God does allow us an abundance, we're to multiply our assets. The late Christian financial counselor Larry Burkett loved to point out that roughly two thirds of the parables that Jesus told were about money and/or multiplying your assets. Money itself is not evil.

> *"Make sure that your character is free from the love of money, being content with what you have;" Heb. 13:5*

In the Matthew 25 parable about investing, some made money, some lost money, but the only guy who was chastised was the one who buried his money and wasn't even earning interest. His failure was because he did not invest.

So it's not wrong to have some savings or even a lot of investments. What's important is to have the right Biblical purpose for which you save. Our life's focus should not be saving money for retirement. Rather, investing in eternity.

Spiritual Maturity Is our Goal

Our desire should be "rich toward God," not spending our lives trying to save enough money to get to a point to do nothing. By making spiritual maturity the goal, when a man is older he will have a lot to offer in wisdom. He can then attest to the fact that this life is all about God, not money. It's about being mature in God's ways, not man's.

> *"They will still yield fruit in old age; They shall be full of sap [Hebrew = lit: fat;] and very green [mature;], To declare that the LORD is upright; He is my rock, and there is no unrighteousness in Him." Psa. 92:14-15*

> *"...until we all attain to ... a mature man," Eph. 4:13*

> *"...they are choked with worries and riches and pleasures of this life, and bring no fruit to maturity." Luke 8:14*

> *"...let us press on to maturity..." Heb. 6:1*

So keep your eyes on the real prize!

CHAPTER ELEVEN

YOU'RE COMMANDED TO KNOW BIBLICAL PROPHECY

At the time Jesus began His ministry on earth, only the Jews were looking for a Messiah. Only the Jews had recorded prophecies from God foretelling of a time that their Messiah would come and rule the world in righteousness.

> *"And the LORD will be king over all the earth; in that day the LORD will be the only one, and His name the only one." Zech. 14:9*

> *"... You will judge the peoples with uprightness and guide the nations on the earth." Psa. 67:4*

But Israel's redeemer had yet to come, and the cruel Roman rule was detested by all of Israel as they waited for their promised Messiah.

The Jewish hierarchy, mostly Pharisees and Sadducees, controlled the theocratic Israeli government and worked with the Roman officials to stay in power. They promised Rome there would be no problems if they allowed the Jews to:

- Worship in their Temple
- Celebrate their feasts
- Make their sacrifices

This partnership kept the Jewish hierarchy in power and prestige. But even though Israel managed to have some autonomy, Rome still had ultimate rule ... and it was a vicious rule. The glory of the pro-Israel days of King Herod the Great, who died in 4 BC, was fading fast.

After Herod's death, his son Archelaus ruled over Jerusalem, Jaffa, and Caesarea for nine years, 4 BC to 6 AD. He acted like a pompous king, wearing all white and sitting on a golden throne.

But even though Israel managed to have some autonomy, Rome still had ultimate rule.

Archelaus made pagan changes to the outside of the Jewish Temple by force. Trying to keep peace, he had his army kill 3,000 Jews. He even canceled an entire Passover! Obviously, he was loathed by the Jews.

With the tax receipts from Jerusalem to Rome dropping and his inability to keep peace and rule effectively, Archelaus was eventually replaced by a prefect appointed by the Roman government.

Pontius Pilate, who was ruling at the time of Jesus' ministry, was the third in a series of these appointed prefects to exercise an iron-clad rule over the Jews in Jerusalem.

Typical Roman coin in 30 AD

Not all the Jews were willing to wait for the Messiah. Between 20 AD and Jesus' death in 33 AD, there were some 60 Jewish insurrections put down by Rome.

The biggest rip-your-robe and throw-dirt-in-the-air of the Roman rules was that they made the Jews use Roman coins—forbidding Israel from minting and using its time-honored shekel.

And adding to the Jewish misery, most Roman coins had a physical image inscribed on the coins. The Jews thought this was blasphemous, due to the second of the 10 commandments.

> *"You shall not make for yourself an idol, or any likeness of what is in heaven above or on the earth beneath or in the water under the earth." Ex. 20:4*

And using a coin with Caesar's picture on it to pay for the mandatory half shekel Temple tax was detestable.

> *"'Show Me the coin used for the poll-tax.' And they brought Him a [Roman] denarius. And He said to them,*

'Whose likeness and inscription is this?' They said to Him, 'Caesar's.'" Matt. 22:19-21a

So by 30 AD the Roman taxes were sky-high and the tension between Rome and Israel was at a fever-pitch. The people in Israel prayed daily for relief as they waited for their Messiah to come. To the Jews this meant the Messiah would come, defeat Rome, and set up His prophesied kingdom.

Messianic Expectations

This was the life and times of the Jews into which Jesus was born. He began His ministry in this tense environment, and to many local Jewish observers, the miracles He performed made Him look, sound, and act like He could be the prophesied Messiah.

This is why Jesus was asked so many times, by a wide range of people, whether He was the Messiah, the King of the Jews. Was He the Messiah? Had He come to set up His Kingdom?

So expectations of a coming Messiah were quite rampant in Israel when Jesus came on the scene. King Herod mentions the future Messiah when the wise men came to Jerusalem looking for the King Who had just been born:

"Gathering together all the chief priests and scribes of the people, [Herod] inquired of them where the Messiah was to be born. They said to him, 'In Bethlehem of

Judea; for this is what has been written by the prophet:'" Matt. 2:4-5

The Samaritan woman at the well mentions the Messiah:

"The woman said to Him, 'I know that Messiah is coming (He who is called Christ);'" John 4:25a

Prior to Jesus' arrest, the Pharisees ask about the Messiah:

"Now having been questioned by the Pharisees as to when the kingdom of God was coming, He answered them and said, 'The kingdom of God is not coming with signs to be observed;'" Luke 17:20

Expectations of a coming Messiah were quite rampant in Israel when Jesus came on the scene.

Pontius Pilate quizzed Him:

"Pilate questioned Him, 'Are You the King of the Jews?'" Mark 15:2a

The two thieves on the cross both mentioned it:

"One of the criminals who were hanged there was hurling abuse at Him, saying, 'Are You not the Christ [redeemer]? Save Yourself and us!'" Luke 23:39

"And he was saying, 'Jesus, remember me when You come in Your kingdom!'" Luke 23:42

Even after Jesus' resurrection, His somewhat still-confused disciples asked Him if He was now going to set up His "kingdom."

"So when they had come together, they were asking Him, saying, 'Lord, is it at this time You are restoring the kingdom to Israel?'" Acts 1:6

But Jesus' incredible miracles were not welcomed by everyone in the land.

It was in this climate that Jesus spent 3 1/2 years healing myriads of sick and lame people all over Israel. He did so much in those few short years that John wrote:

"And there are also many other things which Jesus did, which if they were written in detail, I suppose that even the world itself would not contain the books that would be written." John 21:25

In 3 1/2 years Jesus criss-crossed the Holyland at a dizzying pace, drawing HUGE crowds everywhere He went.

"Jesus was going throughout all Galilee, teaching in their synagogues and proclaiming the gospel of the kingdom, and healing every kind of disease and every kind of sickness among the people. The news about Him spread throughout all Syria; and they brought to Him all who were ill, those suffering with various diseases and pains, demoniacs, epileptics, paralytics; and He healed them. Large crowds followed Him from Galilee

> *and the Decapolis and Jerusalem and Judea and from beyond the Jordan." Matt. 4:23-25*

But His incredible miracles were not welcomed by everyone in the land. The Jewish ruling authorities were at their wits' end. They feared He had grown so well known that if they allowed Him to continue, the populace would inaugurate Him as King and they would lose their power.

> *"Therefore the chief priests and the Pharisees convened a council, and were saying, 'What are we doing? For this man is performing many signs. If we let Him go on like this, all men will believe in Him, and the Romans will come and take away both our place and our nation.'" John 11:47-48*

The Jewish ruling authorities were at their wits' end.

Trying to Catch and Kill Jesus

So after 3 1/2 years, we find Jesus and His disciples walking up the road from Jericho to Jerusalem for the required attendance of the Passover celebration.

> *"Three times a year all your males shall appear before the Lord GOD." Ex. 23:17*

But Jesus stopped short of Jerusalem by a mile or so to spend the night with Lazarus in Bethany.

One week earlier Jesus had raised Lazarus back to life. It was His biggest miracle yet and was performed right under the noses of those who wished to kill Him. Lazarus had been dead for four days—the corpse was even beginning to rot and smell. So there was no doubt to anyone that he was quite dead.

The Roman historian Tacitus said 2,700,000 Jews came for the Passover celebration each year. Since only 350,000 or so could cram inside the walls of Jerusalem, the rest would have to camp in side-by-side tents and makeshift shelters easily stretching as far as Bethany.

Therefore, when Jesus raised stinky Lazarus from the dead, everyone in town heard about it. Raising Lazarus from the dead was still the talk of the town for the millions arriving for Passover that week.

Jesus, knowing the purpose for which He had come to earth, was simply stoking the fires of the Pharisees. They had given the order that if anyone knew where He was, they were to report it so Jesus could be seized and killed.

After raising Lazarus from the dead, Jesus left for one last week, sort of a goodbye trip to Galilee and back, seeing friends and family and performing his last miracles in Galilee and the Jordan Valley.

His last stop was in Jericho, where He healed two blind men and spent the night with Zaccheus, a short but rich tax-gatherer who got saved by believing Jesus was the Messiah.

The next day Jesus departed Jericho on the road to Jerusalem, a day's journey by foot, weaving 23 miles up a total elevation of 3,000 feet through the Judean Desert.

> *"As they were leaving Jericho, a large crowd followed Him." Matt. 20:29*

Jesus arrived at Lazarus' house just before dark on Friday evening as the whole city shut down at dusk for Shabbat. But when Shabbat was over, the crowds came to Lazarus' house... to see both of them!

> *"The large crowd of the Jews then learned that He was there; and they came, not for Jesus' sake only, but that they might also see Lazarus, whom He raised from the dead." John 12:9*

By this time the chief priests had seen enough. The entire town, two to three million people, was talking about Jesus. Was He the Messiah? Would He come to Passover so they could see Him?

> *"So they were seeking for Jesus, and were saying to one another as they stood in the temple, 'What do you think; that He will not come to the feast at all?'" John 11:56*

So in their fearful state of mind, the chief priests somehow determined that killing both Jesus AND Lazarus would solve the problem!

"But the chief priests planned to put Lazarus to death also; because on account of him many of the Jews were going away and were believing in Jesus." John 12:10-11

"So the Pharisees said to one another, 'You see that you are not doing any good; look, the world has gone after Him.'" John 12:19

So the day after Shabbat, Sunday, with the Pharisees seeking to kill Him, Jesus did the unthinkable. He sent two of His disciples to get a colt in nearby Bethphage so He could publicly ride it about a quarter-mile to the top of the Mount of Olives.

"When they had approached Jerusalem and had come to Bethphage, at the Mount of Olives, then Jesus sent two disciples, saying to them, 'Go into the village opposite you, and immediately you will find a donkey tied there and a colt with her; untie them and bring them to Me.'" Matt. 21:1-2

This was a special day. Christians refer to it as Palm Sunday, because the throngs of people lining the narrow street threw their coats down in front of Jesus riding the colt, as well as palm branches they cut from the trees.

"Most of the crowd spread their coats in the road, and others were cutting branches from the trees and spreading them in the road. The crowds going ahead of Him, and those who followed, were shouting, 'Hosanna to the Son of David; BLESSED IS HE WHO COMES

IN THE NAME OF THE LORD; Hosanna in the highest!'" Matt. 21:8-9

This must have been some sight. If they hadn't seen Jesus healing people in their hometowns, they certainly had heard about Him. The crowd would have been in the thousands... which means thousands of coats and palm branches would have been spread over the road.

And with people deliriously screaming "Jesus is the Messiah!" it must have been a celebration atmosphere beyond description. The Jews do know how to party! But there were also Pharisees in the crowd watching all this take place. Again, fearing they were losing their power and influence, they demanded Jesus stop being called "King."

"Some of the Pharisees in the crowd said to Him, 'Teacher, rebuke Your disciples.' But Jesus answered, 'I tell you, if these become silent, the stones will cry out!'" Luke 19:39-40

Jesus made the profound statement that the crowd had to proclaim Him Messiah or the rocks would have to speak out that truth!

This sets up the most incredible fulfillment of Bible prophecy to date. For 3 1/2 years Jesus had discouraged any talk about His being the Messiah. In Caesarea Philippi, when Peter made his famous "You are the Christ" statement, Jesus said yes, He was the Messiah, but not to tell anyone.

> *"Then He warned the disciples that they should tell no one that He was the Christ." Matt. 16:20*

But on this day, things had changed. On this day Jesus allowed, even encouraged, the multitudes to welcome Him as their Messiah. What was different? Why did Jesus say it was now OK to call Him Messiah and/or King?

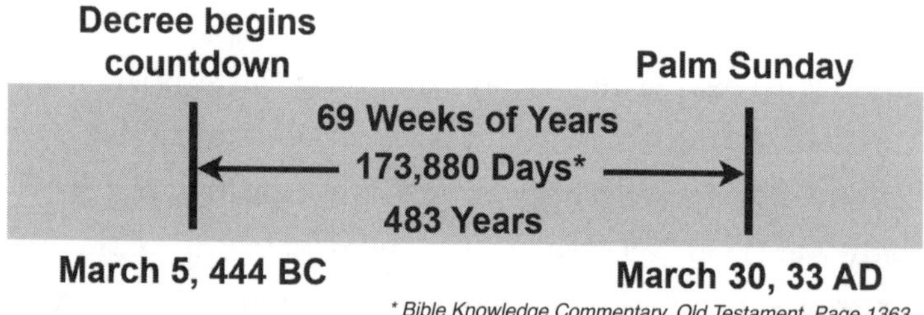

The reason is simple. This was a prophesied day that the Jews should have recognized. The "70 Weeks" (490 years) prophecy given by Daniel had begun to count down 173,880 days earlier.

> *"Seventy weeks (weeks of years, 490 years total) have been decreed for your people and your holy city..." Dan.9:24a*

> *"Then after the sixty-two weeks (483 years from the beginning of the prophecy, 173,880 total days) the Messiah will be cut off (executed)." Dan. 9:26a*

When Jesus got to the top of the Mount of Olives, seeing the Temple in the distance, He dismounted the donkey and cried. The Greek word actually means "sobbed."

"When He approached Jerusalem, He saw the city and wept over it, saying, 'If you had known in this day, even you, the things which make for peace! But now they have been hidden from your eyes.'" Luke 19:41

The Daniel 9:24-27 prophecy was being fulfilled right before the Pharisees' eyes. Daniel had given the exact day the Messiah would arrive. All the Jews had to do was count the days...and this was that day!

But despite the exactness of the prophecy in Daniel 9, the ruling Jewish hierarchy totally missed it! Instead of watching for and welcoming the Messiah, they instead crucified Him.

But the main point is that Jesus was holding the Pharisees accountable for knowing, understanding, and applying Bible prophecy.

Interestingly, the Daniel 9 prophecy wasn't even in the first five books of the Bible (the Torah) that were read completely through once a year on Shabbat (each Saturday). One had to dig a little to find this Scriptural nugget...and think a lot to understand it.

So we should learn a great lesson...Jesus believes Bible prophecy is important! He expects us to know, understand, and apply latter-day prophecies! We'll probably also have to dig a little. But it's important to include it in our overall Biblical study.

Too many churches today are moving away from teaching prophecy, usually saying it's too divisive. Well, Jesus sure thinks it's important. And it broke His heart when the Jews missed His first arrival.

Therefore, we can safely and boldly say that Jesus wants us to know all about the Rapture and His Second Coming! And, as you're probably fully aware, Jesus is coming again! And with some 28% of the Bible actually being prophetically oriented, most Christians should be doing more, not less, study of Bible prophecy! Most importantly, Bible prophecy is an incredible witnessing tool as it gives hope to a hurting world! Jesus is coming as a just and righteous King of the World.

When the Church is raptured, the more people left behind who understand what just happened (even though they didn't believe it at the time), the more likely they'll make decisions that count for eternity. For example, many will "Refuse the Mark"!

Therefore, since we're living in the last of the last days, it's incumbent on us to have a working knowledge of what's ahead. We're to be ready to make a defense of what we believe.

> *"...but sanctify Christ as Lord in your hearts, always being ready to make a defense to everyone who asks you to give an account for the hope that is in you, yet with gentleness and reverence." 1 Pet.3:15*

ISRAEL TODAY

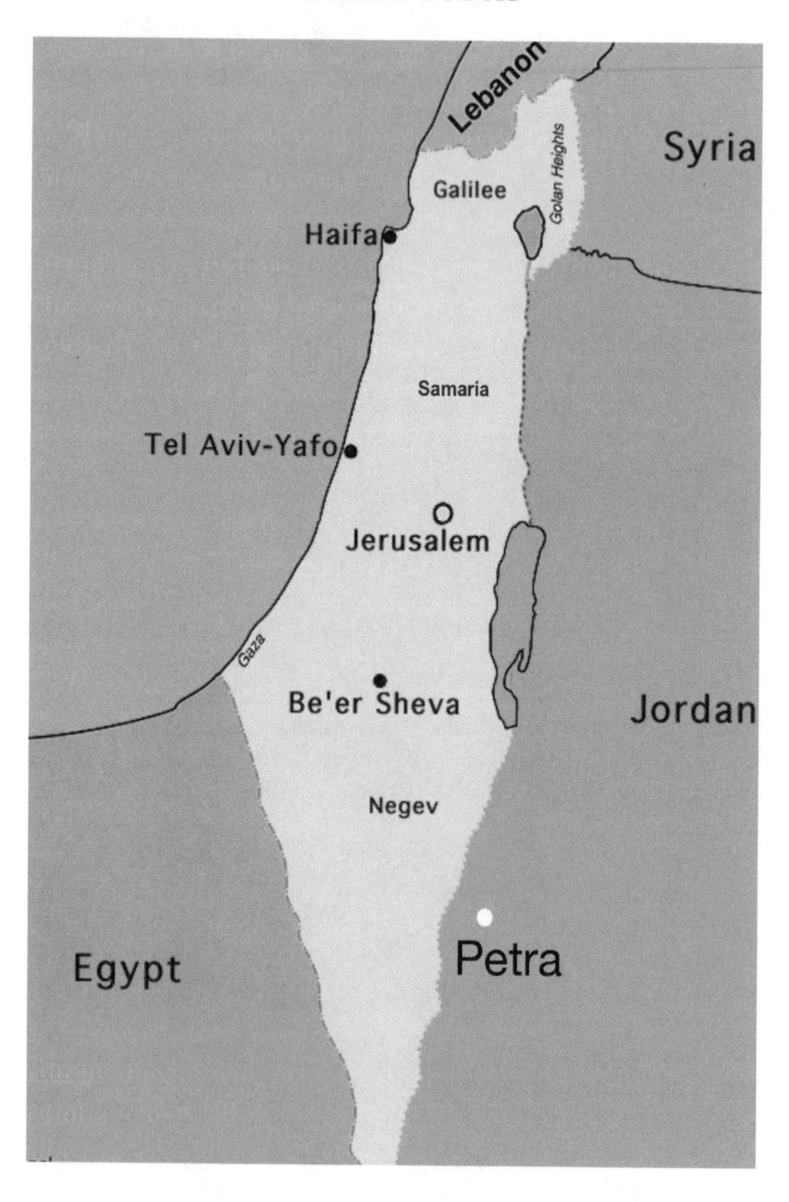

CHAPTER TWELVE

THE PATH TO PETRA

One of the NEW Seven Wonders of the World, Petra is incredibly fascinating—a place like no other. Located in southern Jordan near Israel's border, Petra was once a thriving metropolis. But today Petra is an empty and deserted city with an incredible future destiny.

Though Petra's hard to reach due to the rugged and almost impassable mountains of western Jordan, still almost a million tourists trek there each year from all over the world to see the 2000-year-old, jaw-dropping scenery carved out of solid rock.

This chapter briefly outlines the case for Petra to be the place to which the Jews will flee in the middle of the coming seven-year Tribulation period.

This is the time when we believe Petra will stand tall in fulfillment of Bible prophecy—the last 3 1/2 years of the Tribulation, the length of days described in Daniel 12:11.

The following is a brief explanation of where Petra comes into play in the Tribulation.

Following The Rapture...

After the Rapture, when God removes every breathing Church Age Saint from earth, there is a 50-day period before the Tribulation begins. The 50 days balance the 50 days between the Cross and the arrival of God's Holy Spirit. (For more information see Chapter 15.)

The Post-Rapture Chaos

The phenomenal effect the Rapture will have on the world includes causing the electrical grid to temporarily go down due to the disruption of the earth's magnetic fields...without which electricity won't work. (For more on this refer to pages 4-7.)

Numbing the world, the Rapture will affect every corner of every country. In an instant, people will vanish into thin air without a trace—political leaders, businessmen, rich and poor, workers and unemployed. Everyone left behind will know someone who is missing.

Men and women, husbands and/or wives, parents and/or children will simply be gone. In the U.S. about one out of every twenty-five people will disappear in the blink of an eye. What a mess.

In this post-Rapture, 50-day period with Israel's only real ally—the United States—decimated, Russia sees her opportunity to invade Israel to capture her "spoils," or treasures, fulfilling the remarkable prophecies of Ezekiel 38 and 39.

Today in Israel there are no large spoils to win that would entice a sovereign nation to invade. But whether the Bible is referring to oil fields, gas fields, or diamonds under the Dead Sea, SOMETHING will eventually be discovered that is so valuable to Russia, Iran, and a few other nations that it's worth the risk of starting a world war.

Russia and/or Iran use nuclear weapons in the surprise invasion, but God allows Israel to defeat Russia, including those joining her and Iran in the invasion. The nations of the world will be dumbfounded by Israel's victory.

Men and women, husbands and/or wives, parents and/or children will simply be gone.

With nuclear weapons out of the bag and her only ally in the world helpless, Israel sees her only option is to secure her safety. She begins taking out all the hostile nations around her, decimating one after another.

> *"In that day I will make the clans of Judah like a firepot among pieces of wood and a flaming torch among sheaves, so they will consume on the right hand and on the left all the surrounding peoples, while the inhabitants of Jerusalem again dwell on their own sites in Jerusalem." Zech. 12:6*

With the Muslim nations screaming for their lives and begging Israel to stop the destructive romp, one man will rise up with a plan. He'll convince 10 nations to agree to guarantee a peace plan for Israel for a period of seven years in exchange for Israel halting her military's war machine.

"And he will make a firm covenant with the many for one week [week of years]," Dan. 9:27a

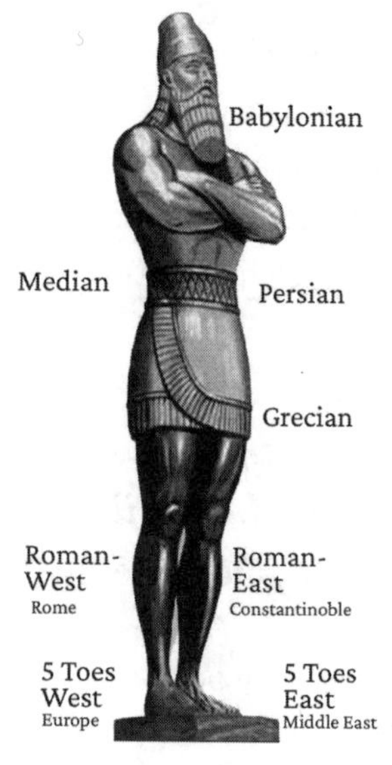

This peace treaty begins the seven-year Tribulation, and "the covenant" will be a peace between five nations from Europe, the western leg's toes of Daniel's image in Daniel 2; and five nations (toes) from the eastern leg of the image (10 toes in Daniel 2:41, 10 kings in Revelation 17:12).

Israel, from a position of strength following their great victory over Russia/Iran, agrees to the peace treaty, which includes the right for Israel to rebuild the Temple on the Temple Mount.

The heralded "two witnesses" in Revelation 11 will show exactly where the Temple should be located. The beloved Jewish Temple will be rebuilt, and the Jews will return to animal sacrificial offerings for blood atonement.

But 3 1/2 years later (Daniel 9:24) the peace will come to a screeching halt when the world leader double-crosses the Israelis, breaks the treaty, puts a stop to the sacrifices, and orchestrates an attempted total annihilation of the Jews.

This evil double-crosser literally murders 10 million Jews in one day, two of every three on the earth. Jesus describes it as the worst day in the history of the Jews—past, present, and future.

> *"...a great tribulation, such as has not occurred since the beginning of the world until now, or ever will." Matt. 24:21*

Imagine, if you can, a single day when two thirds of all Jews will die (Zechariah 13:8) at the hand of the double-crossing Antichrist! In WWII, Nazi Germany murdered six million Jews over four years. This will be about ten million murdered in one day!

Therefore, the worst Jewish holocaust is still in the future! Calling it a holocaust might be an understatement. The horror of this one day is so bad it's actually hard to comprehend.

This takes place at a time when all the Jews in the world will have been forced to squeeze back into Israel, which is not very large, roughly the size of New Jersey. With fifteen million Jews in the world today, that's ten million Jews murdered in one day—certainly qualifying as the worst day in the history of the Jews!

Also in the first half of the Tribulation, 144,000 Jewish evangelists will proclaim the good news of Jesus' shed blood for sins (Revelation 7:4; 14:6). Some Jews will believe the Gospel of Jesus Christ, some won't, setting the fate of millions who die in that one day.

But the focus of this chapter is not the two thirds who die but rather the one third who escape, having heeded the warnings of the 144,000 Jewish evangelists pointing to God's Word.

The following is a simple time-line of events for the middle seven days in the heart of the seven-year Tribulation:

- The Antichrist, having had enough of the two witnesses, tries to kill them. But instead, the two witnesses kill the Antichrist (Revelation 11:5).

- The world mourns the death of the world leader for three days (Revelation 13:3).

- Satan is thrown to the earth from heaven. Satan, being a spirit, needs a body and takes up residence in the body of the dead world leader (Revelation 12:9).

- The world leader appears to rise from the dead after being dead for three days. He has only one eye and one arm (Zechariah 11:17). But this is actually Satan who's indwelling the body of the slain world leader.

- The risen world leader/Satan kills the two witnesses. The world rejoices (Revelation 11:10).

- The two dead witnesses rise up, visibly alive, into the sky (Revelation 11:11-12).

- The Antichrist goes to the Jewish Temple, halts the sacrifices, stands in the Holy Place, and claims to be the Biblically prophesied Messiah (Daniel 11:31, Matthew 24:15).

This is the literal fulfillment of the famous "watch for the abomination of desolation" prophecies of the most important event in the future for the Jews. It is a sign to them to run as though their life depended on it—because it will!

> *"Forces from him will arise, desecrate the sanctuary fortress, and do away with the regular sacrifice. And they will set up the abomination of desolation."*
> *Dan. 11:31*

> *"Therefore when you see the ABOMINATION OF DESOLATION which was spoken of through Daniel the prophet, standing in the holy place (let the reader understand), then those who are in Judea must flee to the mountains. Whoever is on the housetop must not go down to get the things out that are in his house. Whoever is in the field must not turn back to get his cloak. But woe to those who are pregnant and to those*

who are nursing babies in those days! But pray that your flight will not be in the winter, or on a Sabbath. For then there will be a great tribulation, such as has not occurred since the beginning of the world until now, nor ever will." Matt. 24:15-21

Only one third of the Jews will escape death at the hand of the Antichrist. They flee with nothing but the clothes on their backs. Those who are not murdered and escape will eventually make their way to Edom in present-day southern Jordan, in the area of Biblical Bozrah.

Only one third of the Jews will escape death at the hand of the Antichrist.

It is here in Bozrah that God has prepared a place for the surviving Jews to be protected from the Antichrist's murderous hand.

"And the woman [Israel] fled into the wilderness where she had a place prepared by God, so that there she might be nourished for one thousand two hundred and sixty days." Rev. 12:6

"Enter the rock and hide in the dust.... The proud look of man will be abased, and the loftiness of man will be humbled....." Is. 2:10-11a

"Men will go into caves of the rocks, and into holes of the ground" Is. 2:19a

"In order to go into the caverns of the rocks and the clefts of the cliffs" Is. 2:21

For 3 1/2 years, the Jews will live in fear of the Antichrist but will be provided for and protected by God in the wilderness. They will have been stripped of all their earthly possessions...no cell phones, cars, faxes, Internet, or money.

God will provide them with food and water (Revelation 12:6). They will lose their pride (Isaiah 2:11). With all the distractions out of the way, the Jewish people, chosen by God for His purposes, will reacquaint themselves with their Maker.

After 3 1/2 years, at the end of the Tribulation, their Messiah will present Himself to them there in Petra.

"Who is this who comes from Edom, with garments of glowing colors from Bozrah, this One who is majestic in His apparel, marching in the greatness of His strength? 'It is I who speak in righteousness, mighty to save.'" Is. 63:1

"...they [Israel] will look on Me whom they have pierced;" Zech. 12:10

"And one will say to him, 'What are these wounds between your arms?' Then he will say, 'Those with which I was wounded in the house of my friends.'" Zech. 13:6

The Petra Connection

Two thousand years ago, a civilization called the Nabateans sprang up in south Edom, in the area called Bozrah. History doesn't know for sure where they came from or what caused them to disappear seemingly almost overnight. But they lived there for about 300-400 years, continually building and expanding a city that today we call Petra ("rock").

Petra has only one main entrance that is a mile long, roughly 10 to 20 feet wide, with towering cliffs reaching as high as 300 feet. The long, winding entrance, called the *siq*, opens up into open spaces and canyons large enough to hold five million people when fully excavated.

All throughout Petra, the Nabateans carved into the miles of soft sandstone walls. They carved houses, stables, meeting rooms, caves, tombs, and more. The amount of digging into the sandstone is phenomenal, and the beautiful stone edifices still there today are mind-boggling.

My, my, what a coincidence that in the middle of Edom, in the middle of Bozrah, is a place just waiting to be used by God, a place He prepared 2000 years ago! Just as the Bible predicted. I believe Petra is definitely the place to which the Jews will flee to be protected by God in the last 3 1/2 years of the tribulation.

As we mentioned, Petra was recently designated as one of the "Seven Wonders of the World." Few of the tens of thousands who trek to see Petra each year have any clue about the Biblical tie-in. But we try to make visiting Petra an option on every ground trip we take to the Holyland.

Every Believer should go to the Holyland at least once. Seeing what you're reading in your Bible simply changes you. Whether you go with Compass or someone else, it's worth the effort it takes to get there!

CHAPTER THIRTEEN

ALL ABOUT ANGELS

Invisible angels have been all around us humans since the beginning and have been integral in our history. They clapped approval when God created the heavens and earth (Job 38:7). And it was angels who were involved in Jesus' birth events in Bethlehem over 2000 years ago. So let's look at some interesting angel facts.

Angels are fascinating finite spirit (Greek *pneumata*) beings that are mentioned about 300 times in the Bible.

Jesus created everything, so He obviously thought up, designed, and created angels.

"All things came into being through Him, and apart from Him nothing came into being that has come into being." John 1:3

"For by Him all things were created, both in the heavens and on earth, visible and invisible, whether thrones or

dominions or rulers or authorities—all things have been created through Him and for Him." Col. 1:16

"Let them praise the name of the LORD, For He commanded and they [all His angels] were created." Psa. 148:5 (See also Matt. 8:16, Luke 7:21, 8:2, 11:26, Acts 19:12, Eph. 6:12)

Both the word "angel" in the Hebrew, *mal'ak*, and in the Greek, *angelos*, means "messenger." But angels are also frequently used in the capacity of "guardians."

Here are some interesting facts:

- Angels do not die (Luke 20:36).
- Angels are fixed in number (Matt. 22:30).
- Angels can be male or female. The angels in Zechariah 5:9 were women.
- Some angels have wings (Ex. 25:20, 1Chr. 28:18, 2Chr. 3:11, 13; 1 Ki. 6:27, 8:6-7, Is. 6:2, Ezek.10:8, 12, 19, 21, 11:22, Zech. 5:9, Rev. 4:8).
- Angels were created before the world was created (Job 38:4-7).
- Angels were originally created all good (Gen. 1:31).
- Today some angels are still good (Eph. 3:10, Mark 8:38, 1Tim. 5:21).
- Today some angels are bad and are referred to as "demons" (Eph. 6:12, Jude 6, Matt. 25:41, Luke 8:31).
- And some demon angels are really, really bad (2Pet. 2:4, Matt. 8:28-29, Rev. 12:4).

- Angels have rank and order (Dan. 10:13, 21, 12:1, Luke 1:19, Rev. 8:2).

Some angels have specific assignments:

- Power over fire (Rev. 14:18).
- Angel of the waters (Rev. 16:5).
- Angel of the abyss (Rev. 9:11).
- Angel who binds Satan (Rev. 20:1-2).
- Separate righteous from the wicked (Matt. 13:39-40).
- Michael "shouts" at the Rapture (1Thes.4:16).
- Michael is the archangel (Jude 9).
- Gabriel was a messenger to Daniel (Dan. 9:21, 10:12), Zacharias (Luke 1:13-19), and Mary (Matt. 1:20).
- Lucifer/Satan Lucifer was a cherub (Ezek. 28:14).
- Lucifer was created sinless (Is. 14:15).
- Lucifer was a musician (Is. 14:11).
- Lucifer's beauty and splendor corrupted him (Ezek. 28:17).
- Lucifer wanted to be God (Is. 14:13-14).
- Other key passages about the head angel Lucifer/ Satan (Job 1:6, 2:1, Is. 14:3-27, Ezek. 28:11-19, Rev. 12:7-9, 17:8, 9:2). We are all born with Lucifer/Satan as our spiritual father (John 8:44). Therefore, we must all be "born again" to go to heaven (John 3:1-7).
- Angels Are Protectors (Psa. 91:11, Heb. 1:14).
- God uses angels to help believers (Heb. 1:14, Gen. 24:7, Acts 12:15, Psa. 34:7, 91:9-16).
- God uses angels to help God's servants (Acts 5:19, 12:5-11, 8:26, 10:1-7, 27:23-25).

- God uses angels to protect children (Matt. 18:10).
- Angels have intelligence and can reason (Matt. 8:29, 2 Cor. 11:3, 1Pet. 1:12).
- Angels know more about God than humans do (James 2:19, Rev. 12:12).
- Angels have emotions (Luke 15:10, James 2:19, Rev. 12:17).
- Angels have will (Luke 8:28-31, 2 Tim. 2:26, Rev. 12:17).
- Angels observe Christians (1 Cor. 4:9, 11:10, Eph. 3:10, 1Pet. 1:12).
- Angels can appear as humans (Heb. 13:2).
- Angels can bring answers to prayers (Dan. 10:12, Acts 12:5-10).
- Angels have accountability before God (Job 1:6).
- Angels are limited in power, knowledge, and activity (1Pet. 1:12).
- Angels are a separate order of creatures (Heb. 1:13-14).
- Angels will be judged by Believers (1Cor. 6:3).
- Prior to the cross, angels ushered Believers to the next life (Luke 16:22).
- However, today in the Church Age, Believers go directly to be with the Lord when their life is over (2Cor. 5:8).
- Each country has a head demon angel assigned (Eph. 6:12, Dan. 10:13, 20).
- Each local church has an angel assigned (Rev. 2:1, 8, 12).
- Angels' primary ministry is to worship and praise God (Psa. 148:1-2, Is.6:3, Heb. 1:6, Rev. 5:8-13, Job 38:6-7, Psa. 103:20, Rev. 22:9, Rev. 7:1).

CHAPTER FOURTEEN

MURDERING GOD'S IMAGE

"For You formed my inward parts; You wove me in my mother's womb. I will give thanks to You, for I am fearfully and wonderfully made;" Psa. 139:13-14

In the beginning....

The pinnacle of God's mind-blowing, seven-day creation week was humans being made, amazingly, in His own triune image. God created all of these "images of God" to live, maintain, and populate a most beautiful planet.

Not long after the seven days of Creation (where God declared all He had created was "good"), Lucifer sinned and his ultimate destiny in eternal hell was set. His revengeful vileness runs deep, and for 6000 years he's taken it out on humans. This is because being made in God's image is a constant reminder to the devil of his upcoming punishment by God.

The first thing Satan did after he fell from his lofty perch was set his destructive sights on the first humans—Adam and Eve. We now know through our study of DNA that present in those first two people was 100% of the population of all the world. Who you are today came from literally being "in Adam." So you're therefore a co-recipient of Adam's death sentence.

> *"For as in Adam all die, so also in Christ all will be made alive." 1Cor. 15:22*

But God thankfully made our redemption possible through believing the Gospel, the Good News of Jesus the Messiah's death, burial, and resurrection. Humans are graciously given the choice to opt out of spending eternity in hell by believing the Gospel ... trusting the shed blood of Jesus to cover their sin forever.

Not wishing for anyone to be redeemed, Satan does everything in his power to keep humans from understanding Biblical truth. And if they do "believe," resulting in eternal security, the devil seeks to make Believers' lives miserable through his lies. The last thing he wants is a well-grounded, Bible-trusting Believer.

So Satan knows that to do his job best he has to start early...

> *"The sower sows the word. These are the ones who are beside the road where the word is sown; and when they*

hear, ***immediately Satan comes*** *and takes away the word which has been sown in them." Mark 4:14-15*

But then again, why should Satan wait for someone to hear the Word? Why not just snuff 'em out before they have a chance to hear? Why not murder the Image of God before it's even born?

Ancient pagan civilizations like the Incas, the Aztecs, and the Druids were notorious for child sacrifice. In the Old Testament the Ammonites and the Canaanites sacrificed children in the Hinnom Valley outside of Jerusalem. This was done in the name of Molech, which, of course, is just Satan in disguise. Without God they're duck soup for Satan.

But later in the Bible we are dumbfounded to read King Manassah (2 Kings 21:6), King Ahaz (2 Chronicles 28:1-4), King Solomon (1 Kings 11:4-11), and the tribe of Judah were horribly sacrificing their children (Jeremiah 32:35).

God so detested this practice of child sacrifice that He said anyone doing it should be stoned to death.

"...'Any man from the sons of Israel...who gives any of his offspring to Molech, ***shall surely be put to death;*** *the people of the land shall stone him with stones.'" Leviticus 20:2*

Satan the Deceiver

Today, child sacrifice continues in the form of abortion. Make no mistake about it, abortion is child sacrifice.

Mostly done for the god of convenience or the god of money (thinly camouflaged as maintaining a preferred lifestyle), abortion has murdered over 60 million of our most delicate and innocent Americans since the Supreme Court ruled abortion was legal in the landmark Roe vs. Wade case in 1973.

There is no "safe" abortion. And if you want to talk about women's rights, half of those aborted are women.

Even though the yearly number has dropped in half since 1978, today we are still murdering over 600,000 innocent babies each year in the United States—600,000!

Those 60 million lives, had they lived, would have produced at least another 50 million babies that would now be having more babies.

And those numbers are not even counting the technical abortions caused by birth control. I am amazed how few people know that 80% of the time, the pill works as an abortifacient by not allowing a fertilized egg to implant in the lining. Life begins at conception. Everything for life is contained in that union of sperm and egg. If God sees it as a life, then so should we!

> *"Your eyes have seen my unformed substance; and in Your book were all written the days that were ordained for me, when as yet there was not one of them."*
> *Psa. 139:16*

So if you add those technical abortions from birth control to the physical abortions, you would have somewhere around 200 million more people in our population. That number would make this nation quite great again with a booming economy.

But instead of the post WWII Baby Boom followed by their babies producing the Baby Zoom, Satan was able to dupe Christians and non-Christians alike and we ended up with the Baby Bust. White families went from about four kids per family in 1948 to two kids in 2015. [https://en.wikipedia.org/wiki/Mid-twentieth_century_baby_boom]

Medical Problems Caused by Abortion

The medical results from abortions are simply covered up. It is a FACT that abortions cause an increase in sterility, future births being premature, mental illness, guilt, anxiety, alcohol and drug abuse, and even death—up to 10 each year. And the most under-reported of all, a direct link to breast cancer.

None of these abortion complications are mentioned to pregnant women coming to abortion clinics. There is no "safe" abortion. And if you want to talk about women's rights, half of those aborted are women. What about their rights? What would they say if given the "choice"?

We had Abby Johnson speak at a *Steeling the Mind Conference.* She formerly worked in an abortion clinic for several years, "counseling" those coming in the door for abortions. She dutifully told women seeking abortions what she was told to say.

God's design, IN HIS IMAGE, is magnificent! And impossible to be random.

But one day, due to an urgent staffing problem, she was asked to assist on an actual abortion. It changed her life because she saw first-hand that what she had been telling women was an out-and-out lie. Her story is amazing and was made into a movie titled "Unplanned." Every Christian should see that movie!

And if there was any doubt in your mind that abortion is murder, check out the following developmental descriptions. No wonder Planned Parenthood doesn't allow pregnant women to see one single image on an ultrasound machine in ANY of their 650 clinics in the U.S.! They KNOW that if women saw their babies alive in their womb, they would change their mind about abortion!

At just 5-6 weeks of gestation...

Despite being only a quarter of an inch long, her nose, mouth, and ears are already taking shape! Her heart began beating at 20 days and is now beating about 100 times a minute (almost twice as fast as yours) and blood is beginning to circulate through her body. Brain waves have been detectable for at least 2-3 weeks already!

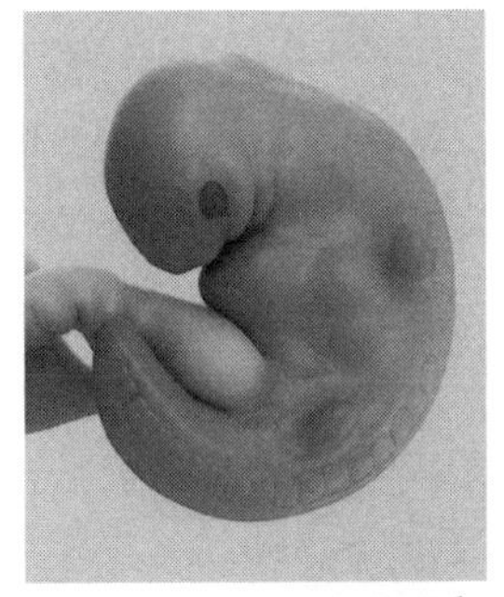
At 5 weeks

At 12 weeks...

Her muscles are beginning to bulk up, as she stretches and kicks. And she'll likely respond to touch because her reflexes are beginning to develop, although mom won't feel it yet.

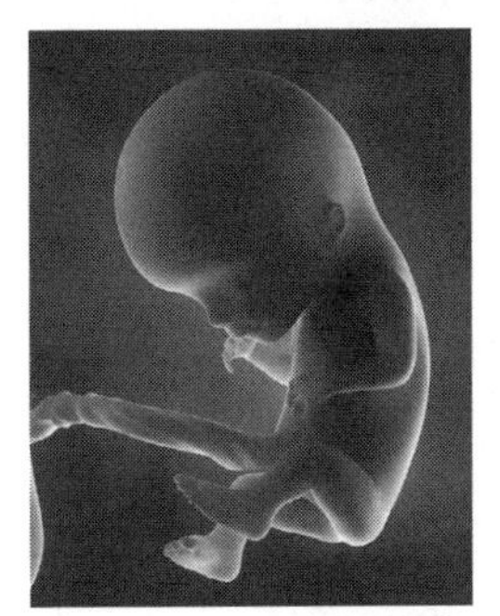
At 12 weeks

At 6 months...

The baby now responds to sound by moving. The mom usually notices some movement, even from hiccups!

Reading these descriptions, I find it almost inconceivable that someone might think life randomly came from two rocks.

God's design, IN HIS IMAGE, is magnificent! And impossible to be random. Giving any credibility to the theory of evolution is simply blasphemous.

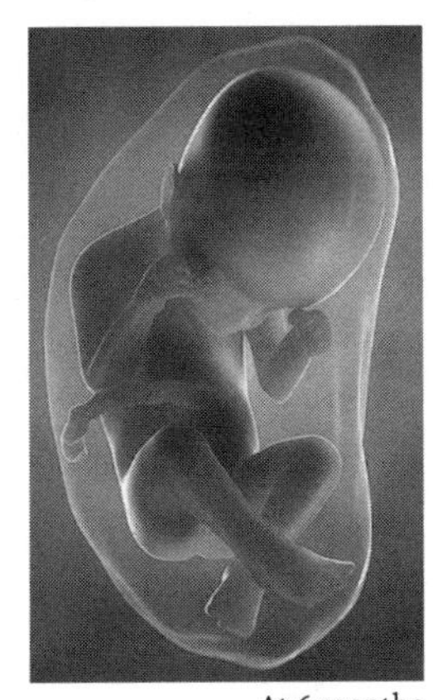
At 6 months

Concluding thought...

If you found out that your next-door neighbors were about to murder their two year old with a knife, would you go to them and try to talk to them? If so, why? What's the difference in a two year old and a baby two months from conception?

The difference is whether or not you look to God as Lord of your life.

> *"...for which I am an ambassador in chains; that in proclaiming it I may speak boldly, as I ought to speak."* Eph. 6:20

CHAPTER FIFTEEN

THE 50 DAYS

BETWEEN THE RAPTURE AND THE BEGINNING OF THE TRIBULATION

The arrival and departure of the Holy Spirit on the earth are the bookends of the Church Age.

The Church Age begins with the arrival of God's Holy Spirit (Acts 2). It is the only time God's Holy Spirit permanently indwells living/breathing humans, who by faith trust in God's Messiah's shed blood for their salvation.

The Church Age ends with the Rapture (the departure of the Holy Spirit from earth).

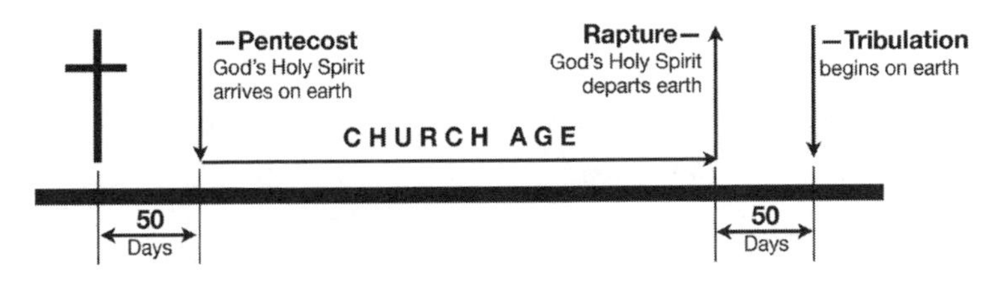

Prior to the Church Age, the time between Jesus' death on the cross and the arrival of God's Holy Spirit was 50 days (see graph above). As balanced as God's Word always is and understanding the incredible importance of the meaning of numbers in Scripture, we theorize that there will be another 50 days between Rapture and the beginning of the Tribulation.

In that brief, 50-day, post-Church Age period, here is what we think has to happen:

- First, God suddenly removes the Holy Spirit Restrainer from the earth (the Rapture).

"...in a moment, in the twinkling of an eye, at the last trumpet; for the trumpet will sound, and the dead will be raised imperishable, and we will be changed." 1Cor. 15:52

"For the Lord Himself will descend from heaven with a shout, with the voice of the archangel and with the trumpet of God, and the dead in Christ will rise first. Then we who are alive and remain will be caught up together with them in the clouds to meet the Lord in the air, and so we shall always be with the Lord." 1Thes.4:16-17

- A coalition of countries led by Russia (Gog) and Iran (Persia) invade Israel for her riches (Ezekiel 38:2-6).

"Thus says the Lord GOD, 'It will come about on that day, that thoughts will come into your mind and you

will devise an evil plan, and you will say, "I will go up against the land of unwalled villages. I will go against those who are at rest, that live securely, all of them living without walls and having no bars or gates, to capture spoil and to seize plunder, to turn your hand against the waste places which are now inhabited, and against the people who are gathered from the nations,"'" Ezek. 38:10-12

- Israel defeats the invading armies in what sounds like an atomic exchange.

"...their flesh will rot while they stand on their feet, and their eyes will rot in their sockets, and their tongue will rot in their mouth." Zech. 14:12b

"For seven months the house of Israel will be burying [Gog's soldiers] in order to cleanse the land." Ezek. 39:12

- Israel then takes it a step further. With her only ally, the United States, decimated by the Rapture, she takes action to rid herself of those who have continuously been at war with her. She systematically begins wiping out the rest of her enemies surrounding her borders.

"In that day I will make the clans of Judah like a firepot among pieces of wood and a flaming torch among sheaves, so they will consume on the right hand and on the left all the surrounding peoples ..." Zech. 12:6

- This brings humanity to the brink of disaster as the whole world realizes that Israel has God with her.

"And My holy name I will make known in the midst of My people Israel; and I will not let My holy name be profaned anymore. And the nations will know that I am the LORD, the Holy One in Israel." Ezek. 39:7

- Out of the smoke and confusion comes the bold voice of a mortal man, a man who will eventually become the Satan-indwelled Antichrist. He outlines a grand plan that will save the world. He will entice Israel to stop the wholesale destruction of her enemies by guaranteeing her peace and safety. He even includes in the framework of the peace treaty the right for her to rebuild the Jewish Temple.

"And he will make a firm covenant with the many for one week [WEEK OF YEARS—7 YEARS], but in the middle of the week he will put a stop to sacrifice and grain offering;" Dan. 9:27a

- At the moment Israel inks her signature on the treaty, the last seven years of the 70th Week of Daniel begin and is outlined beginning in Revelation 6.

That will be one wild 50-day period!

CHAPTER SIXTEEN

WHEN WAS NICODEMUS BORN AGAIN?

> *"Jesus answered and said to him, 'Truly, truly, I say to you, unless one is born again he cannot see the kingdom of God.'" John 3:3*

In no uncertain terms, Jesus tells Nicodemus that he must be born again to go to heaven. This is a most amazing statement as it was made to a Jew living under the Law, who could not be "born again" at that time.

Jews couldn't be born again at that time because Jesus' statement was made pre-cross, and therefore pre-Acts 2, when there was no Holy Spirit on the earth to permanently indwell Believers to make them "born again."

Why then was Jesus telling Nicodemus something he couldn't do? Nick could NOT be born again before the Holy Spirit came to earth in Acts 2. No one could be born again until Acts 2. And Jesus was talking to Nick three years earlier!

Why would Jesus tell Nick he had to be born again to see heaven if he had no chance of being born again until years later?

And Jesus' statement was universal, meaning that needing to be born again to see heaven would apply not just to Nicodemus but to everyone who ever lived.

Since it was impossible to be born again without the Holy Spirit being on the earth, was Jesus saying that everyone who had lived and died in the past were incapable of qualifying for heaven?

The answer to this theological dilemma lies only when one applies Biblical dispensational theology to the question. When we accurately handle the Word, we see that although God never changes, He deals differently with people on the earth, depending on the time in which they lived.

God simply worked one way with those living pre-cross and worked another way with those post-cross/post arrival of God's Holy Spirit. Dividing the Bible that way is classic dispensationalism. (See the dispensation chart on the inside front cover of this book.)

What Jesus said to Nicodemus and what was true for every other Old Testament believer who was saved by faith is that they could not go to heaven unless they were born again. They needed spiritual cleansing.

All Jews knew they were sinful and needed a Savior. All Jews knew the sacrificial system that was in place was temporary. All Jews were looking for their Messiah to permanently atone for their sin.

Therefore, Jews under the Law knew they couldn't be "born again" because of their sin and were waiting for the day that God would provide His Messiah to pave the way.

Their Messiah, Jesus, had to first die and rise again to pay for the sin of those who believed God. Only then could anyone see heaven.

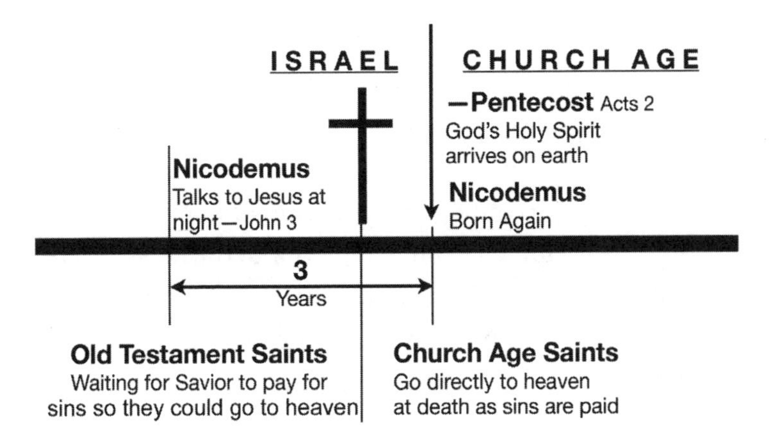

Therefore, everyone in the Old Testament who was saved by faith had to wait to see heaven when they died. So God provided a place called "Abraham's bosom" or "Paradise" for them to reside while they waited.

No one could go to heaven until the Messiah made it possible to be born again.

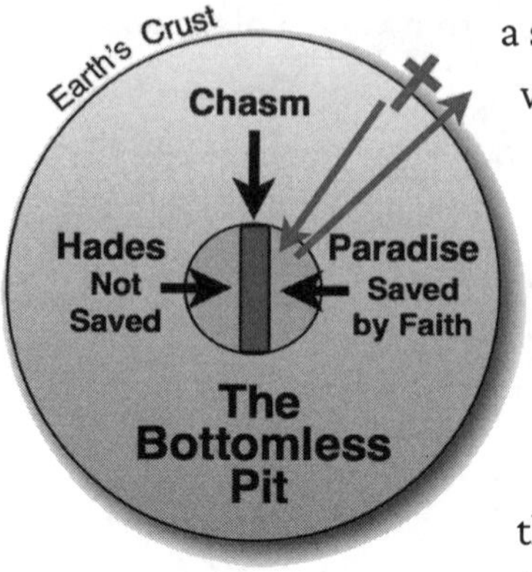

Therefore, “Paradise” was in essence a sort of “holding tank” (it was not purgatory!) in the center of the earth for Old Testament Believers. Here they stayed in this “bottomless pit” and waited for the Messiah to arrive, die, rise again, and therefore atone for their sins so they could go to heaven.

“Paradise” is described in the chilling account (not a parable) of two Old Testament men who died—one going to the Hades side and one going to the Paradise side of the bottomless pit (Luke 16:19-31).

This amazing account gives us a glimpse of what it was like after death for a person living prior to the cross. There were two sides of hell in those days before the cross, one side for those saved by faith in a future Messiah and one side for those who were not saved at all.

Those not saved went to the Hades side, were conscious, and burned constantly in an unquenchable fire. They had memory of their time on earth and longed to be on the Paradise side. But there was zero they could do after death to change the fact they did not believe in a future Messiah.

But those who were saved in the Old Testament, those trusting God for a future Redeemer, went to the Paradise side when they died. Here they waited for God's provision. Abel was most likely the one who had been there the longest, almost 4000 years!

Paradise wasn't heaven, but it was certainly way better than those across a great chasm who had died without faith and now were burning in the unquenchable fires of Hades.

> *"'...between us and you there is a great chasm fixed, so that those who wish to come over from here to you will not be able, and that none may cross over from there to us.'" Luke 16:26*

Imagine all of those saved by faith throughout time, living and waiting on the Messiah. Adam and Eve, Abraham, David, Moses...and millions more, all waiting for the Messiah to come to provide access to Heaven. Fascinating!

And the moment Jesus died on the cross, the gates of hell were instantly opened for all the Old Testament Saints.

They left Paradise and broke through the earth's crust on their way to heaven. It was not until their sins had been PAID that they could be born again. The born-again boom was so great that day that it shook the earth mightily!

> *"And behold, the veil of the temple was torn in two from top to bottom; and the earth shook and the rocks were split..." Matt. 27:51*

At the moment that Jesus died on the cross, the entire aggregate of Old Testament saints was cleansed/born again and released from the Paradise side of the bottomless pit to go to heaven.

When Jesus died, believers made a mass transfer from Paradise.

When Jesus died, this huge group of Believers finally made a mass transfer from Paradise, in the center of the earth, to the real heaven above. As the multitudes broke through the earth's crust on their exciting journey, some even lingered a bit on the earth's surface, to the bewilderment of those still alive on the earth.

> *"The tombs were opened, and many bodies of the saints who had fallen asleep were raised; and coming out of the tombs after His resurrection they entered the holy city and appeared to many." Matt. 27:52-53*

Wow! That sheds a whole new light on the saying, "dead men walking."

A Possible Interaction That Day

Ben sees Joe, a friend who had died several years before, standing in the street and exclaims, "Good grief, Joe, what are you doing here? I thought you died years ago!?"

Joe responds, "I did die, but I couldn't go to heaven until my sins were paid for. But now Jesus, the perfect sacrifice, has made payment for all my sin and I'm headed for heaven now....and look at the time, gotta go, bye." (You have to love God's humor.)

So things had definitely changed when Jesus died. God did not change, but He was changing the way He dealt with mortal man. Before the cross, no one could go to heaven due to his or her sin. Each had to wait for the Savior to make the perfect atonement/provide the perfect sacrifice before going to heaven.

Now, of course, post-cross, when Believers die, their spirits go directly to heaven... made possible because of the shed blood of Jesus.

Now, when Believers die, their spirits go directly to heaven.

"...we are of good courage, I say, and prefer rather to be absent from the body and to be at home with the Lord." 2Cor. 5:8

So in John 3, Jesus was telling Nick a great spiritual truth about the necessity of the payment of His blood before any pre-cross Saints could go to heaven.

Nick must have realized that he could not be born again until the provision was made. He had to wait to be born again until the Spirit of God arrived at Pentecost.

CHAPTER SEVENTEEN

WHEN THE FIRE FIRST FELL

Just after Jesus' death on Calvary's cross, the most spiritually impacting of all dispensational changes occurred ... God's primary focus transitioned from Israel to the Body of Christ—Christians throughout the world.

Eventually this remarkable period, called the "Church Age," will end with the departure of the Holy Spirit, and God will again go back to making Israel His primary focus. But currently, the Church Age in which we live began with quite unique and powerful characteristics.

Here are three evidences of this historical and monumental change that happened in 33 AD.

1. Sinners Gained Direct Access To God

At Jesus' death, the 4 inch thick, 60 foot high and 30 foot wide curtain that ripped in the Jewish Temple from top to bottom, exposing the private Holy of Holies area, was the visual indicator that the blood of Jesus had been accepted as payment for sin. There was now no more barrier to accessing the God of the universe.

It's amazing to think that for some 4000 years, Adam, Moses, Noah, and every other Believer saved by faith through the ages was barred from heaven due to the stain of sin.

Granted, where they waited after death was called "Paradise," but it wasn't heaven. (This was discussed in the previous chapter.)

2. The Holy Spirit Arrives

Just before Jesus departed this earth, He told the disciples to wait for the Holy Spirit to come and permanently indwell Believers. Fifty days after His death, on the Jewish Feast Day of Pentecost, the disciples were gathered in Jerusalem, probably on the Temple Mount.

People have often assumed the "upper room," in the Acts 1 account of choosing a new disciple to replace Judas, was the same room in the Acts 2 account of the arrival of God's Holy Spirit. But a careful reading of the text makes no such definitive assertion.

Acts 2 was definitely a later time than the Acts 1 account when they were meeting in the "upper room," with the 120 people, because the Scripture says:

"When the day of Pentecost had come ..." Acts 2:1a

The last part of this verse continues,

" ... in one place." Acts 2:1c

Although it is usually assumed and taught that this place is the upper room of Acts 1, the text doesn't say that. It only says "in one place." Scripture says it was a place was that could be observed by people seeing the faces of those enough to identify that they were Galileans inside.

The middle part of Acts 2:1 says,

"... they were all together ..." Acts 2:1b

Who is "all"? Referring back to the previous verse, the last verse of Acts 1, Scripture states,

It is usually assumed and taught that this place is the upper room of Acts 1, the text doesn't say that.

"...and the lot fell to Matthias; and he was added to the eleven apostles." Acts 1:26

And in verse 2:14, Peter refers only to the 12 apostles who were present.

"But Peter, taking his stand with the eleven..." Acts 2:14

So I believe it was on the Temple Mount, God's special place on Earth where He first permanently indwelled humans...beginning with the 12 Apostles. He did not concurrently indwell hundreds of people on His initial arrival—only the twelve Apostles.

> *"And suddenly there came from heaven a noise like a violent rushing wind, and it filled the whole house where they were sitting. And there appeared to them tongues as of fire distributing themselves, and they rested on each one of them. And they were all filled with the Holy Spirit and began to speak with other tongues, as the Spirit was giving them utterance." Acts 2:2-4*

This was a loud event... all of Jerusalem could hear the "sound" of God's Spirit's arrival.

This was a loud event...all of Jerusalem could hear the "sound" of God's Spirit's arrival. Then, those nearby the disciples, thousands on the Temple Mount who have gathered for the feast, saw and heard "signs" that this was something new from the Lord.

The three recorded signs of the Spirit's coming—wind, fire, and inspired speech—are considered in Jewish tradition as a sign of God's presence.

- **Wind** (*pneuma*) is associated with God's Spirit (Ezekiel 37:9-14).

- **Fire** from heaven is always an attention grabber (Sodom and Gomorrah, Elijah calling fire down from heaven, etc.).

- **Speech** alterations once began a whole new dispensation at Babel.

So a first-century Jew knew full well this was something very powerful from heaven above. God was making the statement that things had changed. God did not change, but He was changing the way He dealt with mortal man.

"Now there were Jews living in Jerusalem, devout men from every nation under heaven. And when this sound occurred, the crowd came together, and were bewildered because each one of them was hearing them speak in his own language." Acts 2:5-6.

To further establish this "things have changed" moment, God had the disciples each speaking in a different language. Only the disciples were doing this, not the others who were observing the Apostles' strange behavior.

Only the disciples were speaking in other languages, not the others who were observing the Apostles' strange behavior.

*"They [the crowd] was amazed and astonished, saying, "Why, are not all these who are speaking **Galileans**? And how is it that we each hear them in our own language to which we were born?"* Acts 2:7-8

Due to so many people in town for the Feast of Pentecost, there were visitors from all over the Mediterranean. And these visitors were dumbfounded that these men from Galilee were speaking in their native tongues. The Romans, Greeks, Arabs, etc., all heard an uneducated Galilean Apostle of Jesus speaking in their native tongue.

Due to so many people in town for the Feast of Pentecost, there were visitors from all over the Mediterranean.

> *"Parthians and Medes and Elamites, and residents of Mesopotamia, Judea and Cappadocia, Pontus and Asia, Phrygia and Pamphylia, Egypt and the districts of Libya around Cyrene, and visitors from Rome, both Jews and proselytes, Cretans and Arabs—we hear them in our own tongues speaking of the mighty deeds of God."* Acts 2:9-12

The diverse and culturally mixed Jewish crowd was mesmerized by what was happening—and quite curious.

> *"And they all continued in amazement and great perplexity, saying to one another, 'What does this mean?'"* Acts 2:12

It meant things had changed. God had not changed, but He wanted people to know He was changing the way He dealt with mortal man. And it's worth noting that all these men took this story back to their hometowns around the Mediterranean Sea, which was as close as you could come to news going viral today.

3. The Indwelling Spirit

The third evidence that God was changing how He dealt with humans was evidenced by visible observations. The apostles began speaking in foreign languages. Those observing first thought they were drunk. But Peter explained things more thoroughly.

> *"But Peter, taking his stand with the eleven, raised his voice and declared to them: 'Men of Judea and all you who live in Jerusalem, let this be known to you and give heed to my words. For these men are not drunk, as you suppose, for it is only the third hour of the day;'"*
> *Acts 2:14-15*

Peter corrected their assertions of drunkenness and presented them with the Gospel, the good news about who Jesus was, what He did, how He was killed, and that He rose from the dead. It was at this time that individuals responded to the conviction of the Gospel Truth and received the gift of the Holy Spirit.

> *"Now when they heard this, they were pierced to the heart, and said to Peter and the rest of the apostles, 'Brethren, what shall we do?' Peter said to them, 'Repent, and each of you be baptized in the name of Jesus Christ for the forgiveness of your sins; and you will receive the gift of the Holy Spirit.'" Acts 2:37-38*

Peter shared the simple Gospel message that God had sent His Messiah to redeem sinners. If you "believed," your sins would be forgiven and you would permanently receive the gift of the Holy Spirit.

The permanently indwelling Spirit from God, the third part of the Triune God, was now able to live in humans, and He births a new creature on His arrival.

> *"Therefore if anyone is in Christ, he is a new creature; the old things passed away; behold, new things have come." 2Cor. 5:17*

When the Holy Spirit comes into our lives, He illuminates Scripture, heightens spiritual sensitivity, and gives us access to an unequaled power source from above. And therefore lives are changed forever.

> *"So then, those who had received his word were baptized; and that day there were added about three thousand souls." Acts 2:41*

The 3000 people who were saved that day had responded to Peter's invitation to trust/believe what Jesus had provided via the cross. There is no evidence that these new Believers spoke in other languages, known or unknown. Only the 12 Apostles were exhibiting signs.

> *"Everyone kept feeling a sense of awe; and many wonders and signs were taking place through <u>the apostles</u>." Acts 2:43*

Therefore the Church Age began:

- With Jesus' 12 Apostles loudly receiving the Holy Spirit in Jerusalem.

- The event drew the attention of thousands of the Temple Mount crowd, giving Peter the opportunity to share the Good News of Jesus' birth, death, and resurrection.

- Many responded to the Good News and were saved, the same way people get saved today, by believing the Gospel. God's Spirit entered each new Believer, permanently, when he or she believed.

And, just saying, if the Holy Spirit came so very loudly to earth when He arrived and infilled only 12 people, then the Holy Spirit's departure, with millions of Believers in tow, will be ear-splitting!

There will be no doubt to all those left behind that God is again changing how He deals with mankind.

CHAPTER EIGHTEEN

BIRTH CONTROL AND CANCER LINKED

"Behold, children are a gift of the LORD; the fruit of the womb is a reward." Psa. 127:3

On November 21, 2012, *USA Today* ran an article extolling the virtues of using birth control and how it should be available over the counter. It included this quote:

"Birth control pills are so safe and important to women that they should be sold on drugstore shelves, without a doctor's prescription."

The quote was from the American College of Obstetricians. They said their purpose was to reduce unintended pregnancies. They added:

"Oral contraceptives are very safe, and data show women can make these decisions for themselves."

That's a bald-faced lie. Using birth control pills is NOT safe, according to The Mayo Clinic, The National Cancer Institute, and the World Health Organization!

They all have studies that link the increase of breast cancer directly to using the birth control pill. These studies show that women under 20 who take "the pill" increase their chance of breast cancer by an astonishing 820%!

For those who've had an abortion, the percentages are even higher for breast cancer. Unbelievable!

Women under 20 who take "the pill" increase their chance of breast cancer by 820%!

I'm guessing you've never heard these stats before because when I presented this information to our adult Sunday School class, I had people red-faced and livid because they've never been told this before.

I was asked to videotape my presentation in order to get the information out to Christian parents and youth who have never heard these facts.

Obviously there will be those who read this or watch the video who use or used birth control pills, encouraged the use of birth control pills, or know of someone who is living or has tragically died with breast cancer.

If you're in one of those categories, please remember first that God is a merciful God. And also that He has numbered our days before we were born (Psalm 139:16). And He says we can't add one second to our life-span by worrying (Luke 12:25).

So the purpose of this is not to generate fear but to show the truth in an area where many seek to deceive. We only want the facts to be known so people can be wise in their future decisions.

Currently public schools make available birth control pills without parents' knowledge! Parents need to know the truth! And we will tell you the truth in a free video:

Satan's Top Lies – Lie #3: A Smart Family Plans When to Have Children, and How Many

To watch it, go to the **compass.org** store and download it for free. Or you can order a physical DVD to be shipped to you.

A non-profit, non-denominational ministry

Biblelands Cruise

Join us on the trip of a lifetime and make your Bible come alive like never before!

STEELING THE MIND
BIBLE CONFERENCE

Invest a day, reap rewards for a lifetime being taught by top Christian speakers on tough Bible topics.

Good Morning Lord!™

Whoa... who needs coffee! Start your day with a Bible verse and an eye-opening commentary.

The chapters in this book came from our monthly Compass eNews articles—get one free each month!

Creation & the Grand Canyon

Join us and learn the scientific facts about how a global flood formed the canyon only 4500 years ago.

Browse our 300+ awesome video & audio Bible studies recorded from past *Steeling the Mind Bible Conferences*.